Separating, Losing and Exc'
Child en

There is considerable public anxiety regarding the whole area of social exclusion, particularly where children are concerned. This book is about those children who are often socially excluded from schools because they are labelled as having 'difficulties' or 'disabilities'.

Tom Billington looks at the processes of exclusion which rely on restricted and simplistic categories of deficit – 'difficulties' or 'disabilities' – which are often broadly organized as being 'learning', 'social/emotional/behavioural' or 'physical/medical' problems. Using fascinating case studies, the author explores theories of language and experience to show how different narratives are produced which shape decisions about children's lives.

Separating, Losing and Excluding Children challenges our assumptions about children who are labelled as 'different' and questions the truth of expert opinion.

Tom Billington currently teaches in the Department of Educational Studies at the University of Sheffield and also works as an LEA psychologist in the Merseyside region. He has been a teacher and psychologist for over twenty years, working in schools, colleges and universities.

Master Classes in Education Series
Series Editors: John Head, School of Education,
Kings College, University of London and
Ruth Merttens, School of Education, University of
North London

Separating, Losing and Excluding Children

Narratives of Difference

Tom Billington

London and New York

First published 2000
by RoutledgeFalmer
11 New Fetter Lane, London EC4P 4EE

Simultaneously published in the USA and Canada
by RoutledgeFalmer
29 West 35th Street, New York, NY 10001

RoutledgeFalmer is an imprint of the Taylor & Francis Group

© 2000 Tom Billington

Typeset in Sabon by Taylor & Francis Books Ltd
Printed and bound in Great Britain by TJ International Ltd, Padstow,
Cornwall

British Library Cataloguing in Publication Data
A catalogue record for this book is available from the British Library

Library of Congress Cataloging in Publication Data
Billington, Tom.
Separating, losing and excluding children: narratives of difference/
Tom Billington.
p.cm. – (Master classes in education)
Includes bibliographical references and index.
1. Socially handicapped children–Education–Case studies. 2. Handicapped
children–Education–Case studies. 3. Autistic children–Education–Case
studies. 4. Social isolation–Case studies. 5. Child psychology–Case studies.
6. Difference (Psychology)–Case studies. I. Title. II. Master classes in
education series
HV715 .B55 2000
371.9–dc21   00-032832

ISBN 0–415–23088–8 (hbk)
ISBN 0–415–23089–6 (pbk)

To Josie, Daniel, Joanne and Matthew

Contents

Series Editors' Preface

Anyone at all concerned in education at present cannot but be aware of the issues surrounding the suspension and exclusion of children from classrooms or schools. On the one hand we have teachers, ever more pressed in terms of the attainment levels of the children they teach, and more constrained than previously in terms of the content and pedagogy of the curriculum. On the other hand, in many areas we have levels of socio-economic deprivation and drug or alcohol abuse, which have a direct effect upon the disposition and demeanour of the children coming in to school. Parents of children situated in classrooms where the teaching and learning context is disrupted by the behaviour or needs of two or three children request constantly that the education of the majority is not disadvantaged by the behaviour of the few. Parents of children whose needs are very particular, or whose behaviour is erratic or anti-social, argue that their child, as much as any other, is entitled to a broad and balanced education in a situation where they are learning alongside their peers. The issues seem intractable, the arguments irreconcilable.

Tom Billington's book treads a careful path through this minefield of opinion, assertion and sheer rhetoric. He is concerned to return us to first principles, and to enable us to unpick our own assumptions and the, possibly conflicting, theoretical positions which lie behind these. Through analyzing our own attitudes as well as the behaviour and the positions, theoretical and ideological, taken by other professionals, we come to see more clearly how different narratives are produced to justify the subsequent outcomes. Indeed, throughout the book, Dr Billington adopts a narrative approach to the situation. He is concerned both to explicate and illustrate the ways in which the stories are told and documented, from the very informal to the highly formalized and formulaic, act to preclude certain outcomes and facilitate others. He requires us, as readers and as fellow professionals, to render visible the workings of ideology and the subjective nature of language as a feature of the decision-making processes.

In this book, we are presented with many stories. We are always told whose stories these are, related by which protagonists in the drama, and purporting to be about which players. The professionals' 'stories' told, as validated as 'true', by the experts involved, come under the reader's scrutiny, no less than the stories told about themselves by children and parents. But the main endeavour of the book is not to focus upon which stories are true, or which match some supposedly accurate descriptions of objective realities, for it is Dr Billington's assertion that such realities may not necessarily be knowable. For we create these educational or psychological realities in which we work and live, on a daily and indeed a moment-by-moment basis, by the very ways in which we can speak and determine actions. We are all involved, and implicated, in this process – there are no bystanders.

Much of this book rests upon theories of language, and its relation with practice and the construction of reality, which have been much discussed in recent years. Some of these are complex and hard to characterize in terms which are both faithful to the writer(s) concerned and less impenetrable than a London smog! Through the careful use of different types of text, Dr Billington scores high on an accessibility chart, and has used narrative and example to explicate these difficult ideas. This is essential if we are to avoid the trap of over-simplifying a complicated and detailed theory to the extent that it loses not only its explanatory force but also its imaginative originality.

Reading this book can be somewhat of an emotional roller-coaster if the reader has a professional involvement in situations and processes similar to those described in the book. At times, we felt defensive, at times sympathetic, on occasion angry at some part of the process, and on other occasions interested in a more distanced fashion. However, we were always stimulated – stimulated to make sense of the ideas and theories under-pinning this endeavour, stimulated to follow the narratives and their implications through to the end and, most importantly, stimulated to question our own involvement and implication in the 'objective realities' within which these decisions about exclusion and containment are routinely made. The book makes an original and timely addition to educational debate in this area.

Acknowledgements

I would like to thank all the children, parents and their teachers who appear (under pseudonyms) in this book – Gary and his mother; Mary and her mother, Laura; James and his parents; Peter and his parents; John and his mother, May – as well as the many other dedicated professionals who are similarly protected by anonymity. I am, of course, grateful to Wirral Local Education Authority together with the parents and children themselves for agreeing to participate in the original research. The views expressed in the book, however, are those of the author and do not represent the views or policies, either of the LEA or any other agency.

My colleagues from the Psychology Service have provided sources of informed debate, models of professional integrity and also friendship. In particular, I would like to thank Paul Ashcroft and Mark Barrett for their comments on an early draft of the manuscript as well as the office staff for their emergency support!

I would like to thank too the staff at RoutledgeFalmer together with the series editors, John Head and, in particular, Ruth Merttens for the support and advice which has been essential to the successful completion of this project.

I should emphasize the importance of the Discourse Unit in the Department of Psychology at The Manchester Metropolitan University in promoting the circulation of a body of research upon which this book relies. I am also grateful to Professor Erica Burman, and also to Mike, for their continuing personal support.

Finally, I consider my family to be fellow participants and for several years they have endured the consequences of this project. To Josie and Matthew, Daniel and Joanne, my love.

1 Working with Difference

> The difference between the most dissimilar characters, between a philosopher and a common street porter, for example, seems to arise not so much from nature as from habit, custom and education. ... The difference of talents comes to be taken notice of, and widens by degrees, till at last the vanity of the philosopher is willing to acknowledge scarce any resemblance.
>
> (Smith [1776], 1970, p. 120)

Unacceptable Differences

This is a book about differences. In particular, it is about the differences that are looked for in children, the consequent separations, losses and exclusions which they experience and the activities which characterize our professional practices with them.

That all children are different is unsurprising and that we should be interested in these differences, too, seems unremarkable. That we should be interested in certain differences rather than others seems more worthy of attention and analysis. That we should then develop whole industries, technologies and practices in order to measure and manage some specific differences, however, does indeed seem remarkable. For on what basis are certain differences selected for scrutiny? Indeed, whether we celebrate, tolerate or remediate differences are issues which present themselves as a stream of dilemmas throughout our working lives with children.

What are the effects upon the children, therefore, of the professional activities which we select? Indeed, how are we to work with those children, the very nature of whose disease, disability or difficulty we might in itself choose to eliminate, when at some level they may well have an understanding of the consequences which are associated with their difference – the *Separating, Losing and Excluding* which are the subject of this book. Perhaps professional energies might be channelled rather towards practices which seek to minimize some of the more punitive effects of social exclusion.

Public expectations of professionals working with children, however, whether teachers, social workers, psychologists or health practitioners, seem ever to be on the increase. Governments, local authorities and parents are demanding more and more – more work, more skills, more change. Whilst we will be unable to meet all

1

these demands it is clear that professional survival may well depend on our capacities to adapt in a world which, increasingly, expects that its workers react promptly at the behest of fast-fluctuating economic conditions. This book seeks to provide theoretical and practical resources which can support our efforts to make sense of such changing circumstances and support also our endeavours to develop ethical professional practices in respect of the children to whom we devote our working lives.

Origins of a Book

This is a book born out of my work as a psychologist employed by a Local Education Authority (LEA). It is born, therefore, out of my work with other professionals and children whom I meet on a daily basis, all of us seeming to do the best we can, but often colliding (although sometimes embracing) at moments of frustration or distress. Many professionals throughout the various supporting agencies – schools, LEAs, Social Service Departments and Health Authorities – are employed in order primarily to work with children whose differences are considered so significant that they warrant our special attention; for us, then, there can be little energy expended on celebrating our successes. For example, to access my time, other professionals such as teachers have to convince either myself or the LEA of the gravity of a particular situation, or else the severity of a child's difficulties and in order to do this I can be subjected to a litany of problems and stories of failure.

Too often, I thus enter situations which seem irretrievable and I can then experience a further deep sense of unease, which is not only related to the misfortunes suffered by those involved, adults and children, but related also to the ineffectiveness of many of the responses I am permitted to make. Invariably, the other professionals with whom I am involved are kind enough to welcome me into the situation and rarely have I known any direct hostility. The meagre resources at my disposal, however, certainly in terms of available time, place restrictions upon the nature of my involvement and restrict the effectiveness of any resistance to the anticipated social exclusion. Too often, therefore, I enter into a situation when an exclusion of some form (and for whatever reason) can appear to provide the only viable alternative (although sometimes things will have deteriorated to such an extent that any kind of change would provide welcome respite).

For we live in a culture in which children are removed from one school and placed elsewhere just because their differences are deemed unacceptable, although usually there will be a paucity of evidence to suggest that this will result in any kind of success. In this book I consider that such solutions are devised often in accordance with the needs of government rather than necessarily with what a child might choose for themselves, and thus constitute punitive acts of authority in which children's differences are identified prior to the imposition upon them of a social exclusion. I suggest that the effects of such separations may be detrimental and long-lasting, even on those occasions when the child may initially appear as beneficiary.

It is not just children who are affected by such processes, however, for I believe that all who work with children in blaming cultures – social arenas in which children are made to suffer the consequences of their difference – will suffer the effects of involvement. The pathologizing culture in which we live, one in which individuals are made to pay for their own unacceptable difference, affects us all; for a culture in which children are pathologized is a culture which has at its disposal the capacity to pathologize the adults too, parents, teachers or psychologists, for example.

I suggest, too, that the culture in which we live and work is a culture in which the authentic nature of our experience is challenged constantly and the physical demands placed upon us for more and more (whether change, work or skills) can make it virtually impossible for us to retain ownership of our experiences in our daily work, whether commonplace or epic for example, and can thus exhaust our capacities for authenticity. I hope, therefore, that this book can support fellow professionals by its searching for adult qualities and also by its insistence that children too, whatever the nature of their difficulties or disabilities, may also know moments of profound experience and authenticity. As such, I hope that my efforts to find ways of telling stories about children in this book might not only encourage a determination to preserve our own sense of the profound but also help to encourage that sense in all the children with whom we work. For it is the assaults upon the knowledge and ownership of our own experience in our professional lives and places of work which this book endeavours to resist. I suggest that we can most effectively support ourselves in our work by resisting the culture of blame which pathologizes children's unacceptable differences and which can otherwise lead to lifetimes of separation and fragmentation.

Ability and Pathology

On occasions, it may appear to the reader that the text of the book moves away from the sites of practice and towards mere theory or even philosophy. At such times I would plead for patience, however, because always the aim will be to link such passages back to practical situations. It is a tenet within the book, however, that theory *is* practice (see Burman et al., 1996) and that by practising theory we can change our professional practices.

One such theory which underpins many of our current practices with children concerns the concept of ability and a book about children's differences is drawn inexorably to discourses, not just of ability but by definition, also of dis-ability. Indeed, I suggest that children's abilities and, in particular, their intelligences and potentials to learn provide sites for many of the theories and practices which are used often to justify their ultimate removal and exclusion from various arenas of social activity. I suggest here, however, that many of the models of ability, intelligence and learning are themselves limited and that more dynamic representations are necessary in order that we might access the ways in which learning can occur.

Now I do not deny that differences exist between children; nor do I claim that differences do not occur in their talents and intelligences; on the contrary; but perhaps the prevailing culture in which reductionist models of abilities and differences are allocated encourages models more suited to physical or medicalized problems – 'The practice of diagnosis is not appropriate to human difficulties' (Parker et al., 1995, p. 62).

Neither education nor psychology, of course, are responsible solely for any of the injustices which might be represented in this book, for governmental processes are many and complex. However, in part, I write here because of five young people whom I have known – Gary, Mary, James, Peter and John – and because of the ways in which their very being seems to be restricted by the kinds of stories which professionals write about them. I will endeavour not to restrict representations of their humanity to arid narratives of 'difficulties' but place them alongside richer, more vivid descriptions of intelligence from which they would often tend to be excluded. Indeed, it is a premise of the book that there are forms of expression which are more able to conceive of, and which can re-present the range and intensity of human experience. One aim, therefore, is to resist the injustice of being perceived essentially, and in a way which assumes authority over all other characteristics and intelligences, as a pathology or 'handicap' (see Sinason, 1992).

Structure

The book, therefore, seeks to encourage certain ways of thinking about, speaking about and writing about children who are perceived as different. I hope that, eventually, the book might contribute to the emergence of new professional practices by resisting the culture of individualized blame (whether directed towards children or child professionals) and by resisting too the ghettoization in which many children and adults too can currently become detached from some of the big ideas and possibilities of life.

Following this opening, Chapters 2 and 3 are linked around the issues of power which are raised throughout the book. Initial consideration is given to some of the processes which, I suggest, permeate many professional practices which are directed towards children, for example:

- the ways in which various individuals and 'populations' can be identified, separated and excluded from areas of social life;
- the ways in which various individuals or 'populations' can either be seen, written about or else pathologized;
- the ways in which individuals, including professionals, can act to resist within some of these processes.

It is argued that power relations are reproduced within everyday acts and interactions, no matter how inconsequential they may seem, and that they can be reproduced also, not only within the more clearly recognizable professional processes and practices (for example, such as those performed by teachers, psychologists and social workers) but also in all of the social relations which are generated by forms of institution and government.

Chapter 2 begins to address these issues through a narrative style which attempts to communicate something of the messiness of everyday social situations rather than claiming an absolute veracity of events. The ensuing dilemmas which occur in the relations are introduced in a case study which has been taken from my work as a psychologist practising within the education system. The chosen case study is of Gary, a 15-year-old boy for whom the Local Education Authority sought 'psychological advice' from me as part of a 'Formal Assessment of Special Educational Needs' under the 1993 Education Act. The stories are reconstructed from recollections, reflections and also 'field notes' (Walkerdine, 1990) made at the time.

In contrast with the style of narrative adopted in Chapter 2 and its individualized stories of experiences, Chapter 3 focuses on the nature of power relations and the activities of government. In so doing, I look to place some of the professionalized activities on a larger, historicized canvas upon which those activities are connected to the institutional demands of government. Just as Chapter 2 situates the processes of exclusion in the stories of individual people and events, Chapter 3 locates its own narratives of exclusion within the changing histories of particular forms of governmental activity, for example, 'how psychology [and education] functions within current institutionalized structures of inequality' (Burman, 1994, p. 1).

Many of the key theoretical issues which present themselves during Chapters 2 and 3 are only introduced prior to further consideration later in the book. The essential frameworks which inform the questions of subjectivity, power and narrative are provided by recourse to historical and also discourse analytic texts, in particular, Foucault (1967, 1977), Rose (1989), Parker (1992), Burman (1994), Billington (1995).

In Chapters 4 and 5, the claims to truth made through language, narrative and representation are examined and the contributions to the processes of separating and excluding which are made in professional accounts of child psychopathology are considered. The reader is introduced to representations of 'Mary' and 'James' and the ways in which certain words and linguistic practices contribute to particular outcomes for them. Questions raised through recourse to history and language are organized within a broadly discourse analytic approach. These chapters, however, rely on modes of analysis and also ideas about speaking and writing which are derived from seemingly diverse sources including Genette, Lacan, Berger, Bion, Newman and Holzman.

In Chapters 6 and 7 the book attempts once more to juxtapose particular practices and also the sites in which children can be located within a broader, world history, doing so by referring again to my own professional work and experience. The process of 'reading' political economy is begun and Adam Smith, Karl Marx and Eric Hobsbawm are often invoked as political and historical commentators in their respective centuries. The works of Lev Vygotsky and Robert Hinshelwood then support important links between social, political and psychological arenas in the late twentieth century and, once again, particular modes of analysis are suggested (for example, 'alienation', 'object-relations').

Chapter 8 provides the reader with some short experimental representations of individual children prior to employing psychoanalytic readings, which are adopted here for the possibilities which they can offer, not only for relocating individuals within their social conditions but also for resisting the processes of simplistic, individualized pathologization. Specific ideas and practices here are derived from, principally, the works of Bion and Hinshelwood but also the writing of Donna Williams (who has a diagnosis of autism) and are again applied to case studies taken from my professional practices as a psychologist working within the English education system – Mary and James once more, but also Peter.

The book concludes by considering some of the outcomes of the various cases in the book and also by suggesting bases upon which resistances can continue to be developed and which can challenge the prevailing culture in which the separating and excluding of children occur through the pathologizing discourses of stigmatized differences.

Endpiece

The theoretical models throughout the book demand that the reader does not view accounts of indiviual actions as factual but rather as representations as they are a means only of bringing critical illumination to the social processes in which all our professional practices are embedded. Indeed, it is important to note here that, as practitioner, I now operate within the context of a successful LEA which has many good teachers and schools together with well-respected officers and support services.

For it is the industrialized processes of accounting for difference which can too often lie unobserved in our activities with children and, in particular the ways in which such differences can be infected by the practices of pathologization in order to serve economic and political exclusions. It is the intention, therefore, to provide the reader with a range of theoretical tools which can be utilized to analyze these processes of social exclusion in action. Utilization of these resources (primarily history, language, discourse analysis and psychoanalysis) may lead, hopefully, to the emergence of activities better able to resist the punitive and discriminatory consequences of those practices which can be found in education and psychology as well as in other arenas of government, both for the children and for the professionals themselves.

I suggest that the nature of much of our current thinking about children's own thinking and intelligences will one day be considered primitive and I am sceptical, therefore, of professional positions which too easily claim, firstly to know and secondly to blame. The poet Les Murray provides a cautionary tale for all of us who work with children, writing here as a parent, and of a meeting which took place between a child professional and his autistic son and in which we can detect the demise of old knowledge:

> Giggling, he climbed all over the dim Freudian psychiatrist who told us how autism resulted from 'refrigerator' parents.
>
> (Murray, 1998, p. 430)

2 Gary – A Formal Assessment

> A whole army of technicians took over from the executioner, the immediate anatomist of pain: warders, doctors, chaplains, psychiatrists, psychologists, educationalists; by their very presence near the prisoner, they sing the praises that the law needs: they reassure it that the body and pain are not the ultimate objects of its punitive action.
>
> (Foucault, 1977, p. 11)

This chapter introduces the reader to some of the book's recurring themes. In particular, issues relating to the care and control of children are situated in an educational context – the Formal Assessment of Gary's special educational needs. The various reconstructions taken from my assessment, whether of people, events or processes are based on conversations with Gary, his mother and teachers which were recorded at the time (see Billington, 1997). These exchanges are interspersed with additional commentaries and theoretical points and readers are asked to move quickly from the simple to the complex, from the philosophical to the concrete and from the author to representations of the clients.

Formal Assessment is the term given to statutory processes, currently under the terms of the 1996 Education Act, in which professionals from across different agencies are required to provide 'Advice' to LEAs in respect of a child's special educational needs (SEN). A Code of Practice (1994) exists which outlines five different stages of assessment. Stages 1–3 are co-ordinated by individual schools whilst the Formal Assessment procedures are only initiated by LEAs at Stage 4. Teachers, doctors, social workers and psychologists are just a few of those required to provide the Advice at Stage 4 following which an LEA may make various decisions about an individual child. A Statement of Special Educational Needs might be issued, a legal document which specifies a child's difficulties and the measures to be taken in respect of those needs, for example, which can affect their access to further resources or lead to a change of provision.

Nation states in which people are organized according to a capitalized division of labour[1] are host to complex forms of regulation and government. Institutions and forms of work have emerged during the last two hundred years or so in which certain people are licensed to provide truths regarding aspects of other people's lives, for example, professionals in education, health, social services. In my own work as a psychologist, for example, conducted primarily within the educational domain, I am paid to write authoritative accounts of children and in this chapter I describe aspects of an assessment I was asked to conduct on Gary, a 15-year-old boy. Now whilst I am asked to provide truths for such children as Gary, however, it can often be over-looked that I am allowed to evade those questions of truth in myself and indeed, I am required to suspend any search for my own truths. Is it possible to speak a truth of others, though, if I lose sight of truths within me? And yet I am a liar.

One for the Road – Assessments and Lies

> *'Hello Tom, it's nice to see you. Would you like a cup of coffee?'*
> *'Hello, Chris. No thanks, I had one just before I left the office.'* (lie)

In the first moment of contact with Chris (a teacher at Gary's new school) was a spontaneous lie for I had not just had a drink at the office. So why had I bothered to lie?

Words do not necessarily speak for themselves, for they can contain meanings which are not necessarily reducible to single, lexicographical definitions. The lie, therefore, as with any 'word', can betray the existence of other meanings, or 'truths' which, for whatever reason, I was trying to suppress. I suggest here that the seem-ingly innocuous lie, contained in an everyday exchange, hid weightier matters and ideological dilemmas (Billig et al., 1988).

The justification I employed for rejecting Chris's offer, *'I had one just before I left the office'*, may well have been an opportunist move to conceal other meanings which were alive in that interaction and it is likely, as I perceive it now, that forces were at work which were rejecting something other than the actual cup of coffee and which could have been sufficiently dangerous as to require concealment. I suggest here that within the act of rejection stirred the life of an act of 'resistance'.[2] It could perhaps have been directed at Chris personally but s/he did not seem to arouse in me any strong feelings of dislike, rather the opposite. It does seem, however, that I was rejecting something which I connected with Chris, some object which I perceived that s/he represented.

Initially, the object of my resistance could have been the professional conspiracy which often presents itself in the course of my work. Opportunities for professional conspiracies appear so frequently (sometimes in the name of 'Partnership') that any efforts to resist them are always likely to be overcome at some point. I suspect that I collude both willingly and unwillingly on many different occasions in ways which I fail to recognize, or on occasions when I fail to see the possibilities for further resis-tance. On this occasion, however, I had found a tiny resistance and had, therefore, lied. I suggest that this lie was a resistance against a constant feature of my employ-ment – the lure of exclusionary acts – and here I was being invited to participate in the removal of Gary. Both the object of my resistance (the exclusionary practices) and also the resistance itself had thus been disguised by the layers of meanings.

Making visible the minutiae of everyday social occurrences is a laborious task, one which gives rise to almost endless possibilities. At the particular moment when I was refusing the drink, my resistance had seemed both spontaneous and unproblematic. Its singular performance, however, could have masked many different feelings and thoughts which would otherwise have remained unobserved and whose significance would otherwise have been denied.

Dilemmas and Resistances in Everyday Practices

I argue that my refusal of the coffee contained a resistance against the prevailing social power relations which operated between Chris, Gary and myself. Perhaps I was even hoping to show that I could diminish my own powerful position in relation to Gary. As such, it then becomes possible to see that the lie could have been a disguise for a personal gratification which, in its resistance against the power represented by Chris, acknowledged the disempowerment represented by Gary. In such ways the tiny, seemingly inconsequential and casual everyday occurrence might thus be host to a range of issues related to interactive processes and relationships generally, and I argue that professional relationships can hold a constant stream of such possibilities and individual dilemmas.

The inherently social nature of these dilemmas, however, whilst experienced by individuals, provides a dense weave of common, shared beliefs and attitudes which individuals must negotiate and through which decisions will be made. Such dilemmas permeate specialist processes (e.g. educational or psychological domains) but they can also confront us in familiar or apparently mundane situations (NB 'the dilemmatic aspects of everyday thinking', Billig et al., 1988, p. 143).

Such dilemmas, therefore, are seen within everyday acts and relationships and are also reproduced by, and made visible within, the more specifically institutionalized assessment processes. For example, it would not be Gary, the child subject, the supposed beneficiary of assessment, who had the power to request either the assessment, or else the psychological advice (knowledge) for which it is often assumed that I am paid. Neither would it be Gary who determined his own 'needs'. It would not, therefore, be Gary who had the power either to greet me at the door, or even offer or share a drink with me. Such power lay with the teacher, Chris, and it is that power from which I shrank, perhaps, not least for the moral issues concerning my own position.

Of course, refusing a cup of coffee can quickly appear as a feeble resistance, an indication perhaps of what some might see as an unprofessional unease, uncertainty or muddled thinking on my part; but then adhering to the belief in the concept of an 'independent assessment' might itself assume similar characteristics following critical analyses.

The refusal of the coffee could have been, in part, a concrete attempt to restrict the extent of (a resistance within) the available social, power relations. In order to employ such resistance throughout my day-to-day practices, I try to keep alive analyses of the siren voices which can obscure the power relations and the dilemmas, and which in this case were manifest in a teacher's offer of a coffee and a quiet life. These voices can often seduce me to suspend my own intelligences, for they are voices which, in return for my acquiescence, offer a safe passage. To refuse such offers, however, can be difficult for resistance can be dangerous.

Somewhere inside that seemingly insignificant act I seemed to have assumed that the whole process of psychological assessment itself (which is much more than my acts) constitutes a potentially punitive event, and one which would be harmful to Gary. Initially, this may seem an extreme position but it has often been all too easy to detect within assessments the policing and legitimizing of the boundaries of social confinement. Indeed, too often it has seemed worse, and at times I have suspected that I can also be a perpetrator of more brutal crimes against humanity. In that tiny refusal of the coffee, therefore, was the enormity of the conflict stirred (so to speak!) by the prospect of those actions, a defence against horrors within and without. As a conflict which I experience, I can refer to it as one which has an inner, subjective or intra-psychic life. I argue, however, that the life of the subjective experience here would be umbilically connected to external relations, the conditions of which might further prompt my own social responses, in this case contained in the refusal of coffee.

> *'Would you like anything else? Tea ... sit in the staff room for a few minutes? Get your breath? It's almost break time.'*
> *'No thanks Chris, I'm fine.'*(lie)
> *'Right, then, what would you like to do first?'*
> *'Oh, I thought that I might see Gary in his class and then take him out and do a little work with him. Then perhaps have a chat with his teachers ... or anyone else who you think might be relevant ... '*
> *'Well, as I say it's break time now so if you would like to wait? Or if you wanted you could see Gary in the yard. I know, come with me. We'll go upstairs and with a bit of luck we'll be able to look down on to the yard and be able to see Gary up to his tricks.'*

I hadn't known for certain but it seemed as though a 'truth' which lay inside my lie had just revealed itself. Just as my lie to Chris had seemed to conceal other meanings, it seemed that in *'tricks'* s/he too was keeping alive other meanings and dynamics, and I interpret *'tricks'* here to have meant Gary's bad behaviour. The earlier analysis of my lie makes possible now a knowledge of another lie. For I suggest that within a Formal Assessment of a child's needs, it can be adult needs which can take precedence. For example, the 'truth' which may have been concealed within this request for a Formal Assessment (one visible antecedent of the whole process) was the need for Gary to be removed from 'Mill House School'. The offer of a drink, perhaps, had been 'one for the road', a drink for me in anticipation of the road for Gary. Perhaps I had known that before the lie could be detected in Chris's *'tricks'*. Perhaps I must even have known it before refusing the coffee with my own lie.

Gary II – Professional Games

> *'Now if we look through here we should be able to see Gary. If he's true to form we shouldn't be able to miss him.'*

I accuse myself. I have always liked Chris but perhaps I am giving signals that I will conspire – perhaps I have done so in the past.

> *'Mind you, he probably won't do it today. Yes, there he is! Now look, he's the biggest lad, there in the middle, the one with the ball.'*

The boy who had been pointed out to me was in the middle of a group of girls and was just about to throw a 'basket' – a good shot. In order to perform our clandestine operation, Chris and I peered out from a classroom window, but rather than seeing Gary, I began to see a large room empty save for two people in the corner making sparse, hushed conversation, huddled together on tip-toe and swaying awkwardly; they seemed to be peering through some blinds looking for something outside.

If it hadn't been so serious – I knew the game well, Gary was about to be removed from the school – it could have been farcical. But whilst Gary was at play below the sneaky observers had created their own more sinister playground. Chris and I could have seemed ridiculous but I looked at myself and felt shame. Was this the psychologist conducting a scientific 'observation'?[3] If so, then the applied psychology, the science, could not merely present as ridiculous but could also be seen to harbour the same possibilities for malevolence shared by the adults in their calculating reveries.

A boy (presumably the 'other' boy) ran hard at Gary from behind and jumped on his back. Hadn't Chris better get down to the yard and intervene? Well, as the other boy jumped off his back with some force, Gary just gave a playful shrug; it seemed to me to be a routine kind of event between friends which seemed casually to acknowledge something of their relationship. Gary was not moved to react with the expected aggression and which had by now (my own resistance had been pierced) also been anticipated by me.

> *'That was good, Chris.'*
> *'Mmm. That's strange.'*
> *'He reacted really well there … '*
> *'He doesn't normally react like that.'*

Twenty-four hours before, the case had seemed quite different.

Gary I – Meeting 'Mrs Smith'

By the time I arrived at Gary's home on the previous day, I had already had the chance to look quickly through the thin case file. There had been a social worker's report written several years ago (Local Authority – 'LA 1') which primarily concerned Gary's sister but which also indicated that Gary too may well have been sexually abused by their step-father as a young child. The report, however, had advised that at that time all three of the children could be taken off the Child Protection Register. The same authority had also asked one of their psychologists to produce an assessment report on Gary (when he was 6) and his 'learning difficulties' were duly confirmed by the full weight of government in an LEA 'Statement' of special educational needs.

The next item in Gary's file was another 'Statement', this time produced just one year ago by another Local Authority about 100 miles away, 'LA 2'. This account of Gary's 'needs' not only restated his learning difficulties but also hinted that there were some behavioural difficulties to consider. The only other item in the file was a letter from Gary's mother, informing my employing education authority, 'LA 3', that the family would be leaving 'LA 2' during the summer and requesting school placements for all three children in our area '3'.

> '*Mr. Billington? Come in. Would you like a cup of tea? The kettle's just boiled.*'
> '*Hello, Mrs Smith. No thanks, I had one just before I left the office.*' (lie)

The same lie again but perhaps these words contained different 'truths', born of a reluctance to take a drink in any of the houses which I visit. This refusal of a drink had the quality of an insult, for I wanted to avoid the possibility of drinking from unhygienic cups.

I told Mrs Smith that I was employed by the local authority to provide them with 'Psychological Advice' regarding Gary's 'needs'. Now wherever the law allows me to intercede on behalf of people who lack structural power, the power either to demand what might be possible, or else even the power to suggest what might be in their own interest (and wherever I have the will to engage) – I sometimes choose to do so along with, no doubt, many colleagues and other professionals from across the various agencies. However, the disadvantaged in social power relations can be the recipients of well-meaning resistance and I can often fail to see either the power of my own position, holding as it does the possibility of such benevolence, or else can fail to see the quicksands underneath the beckoning high moral ground.

> '*Could I see Gary?*'
> '*He's in school.*'
> '*Oh, I didn't know. Where is he then?*'
> '*He started at Mill House in September.*'

Information in the file had not included any intended school placement but Gary had been put into a unit designated 'special' for children with 'complex learning difficulties'. To all intents and purposes, however, Mill House was still a unit for children who might in the past have been labelled as mentally retarded – children whose difficulties are often perceived to be anything but complex.

> '*So how does he get there?*' (Mill House is several miles away)

> '*He goes on the ordinary service buses.*'
> '*Does he?*'

I was surprised. That Gary should go voluntarily seemed to speak of his initiative, social competence and also indicate at least some willingness on his part to participate positively in the education process.

> '*Yeh, he goes every day. I know he's high-spirited but that's just his way. You see we've been through a very difficult year. I found out that my husband, Gary's step-dad, was abusing my daughter ... Social Services investigated it all and they said that she had been abused but the police wouldn't be able to prosecute because the evidence wasn't there to get a conviction ... Now Gary takes after me, he's dyslexic. I could read but I was no good at school. He's a good lad but his dad was always rough with him, you know in telling him off ...*'
> '*Right then, are you happy with Gary being in Mill House then?*'
> '*Oh, he loves it. As I say he has his ups and downs and he did get suspended just before half-term but I've had a chat with [Chris] and it's all settled down now.*'

Gary III – Professional Practices and Discourses of Intelligence

It is difficult to accept that, in our supposedly 'advanced' society, children continue to be removed from their local community in order to attend institutions outside of their social sphere, especially when this is justified on the basis of a partial and overly simplistic view of their abilities and intelligences. Large numbers of children are not educated in their home community, and different reasons are made available by professionalized discourses in justification (e.g. either through exclusion or SEN). I often meet such children years later and only rarely will they have been allowed back into mainstream school. The eventual reasoning usually claims that it would either be too late for those children to change schools or else that nobody had known before that they were so able; or, that the children couldn't survive in a mainstream school, either because they couldn't read or else because they were so 'vulnerable'.

Now all children who do not attend their local community school will, at some point, have been taken out of a particular social sphere and perhaps separated from their first friends. This, of course, is not only of structural concern, for it is a process which affects the lives and experiences of all the participants. Both Mrs Smith and Chris knew of this process well and will have spent portions of their lives dealing with that knowledge in their own ways. Gary and other young people in the school were now receiving their training. In refusing the first offer of a coffee (the 'lie') I was desperately trying to hold on to my own intelligences for at times it can begin to seem that the denial of intelligences becomes a social discourse/practice/myth in which we are all invited to participate.

Face-to-face and alone with one another for the first time, Gary and I both seemed wary of one another. I wondered whether he had questions concerning the kind of stories about him already told to me by his teachers, and I wondered perhaps whether he had thoughts about the purpose of my visit.

I also knew by now that the Formal Assessment had been initiated, not on account of his supposed 'learning difficulties', but because of his reported behavioural misdemeanours (this point was to become crucial). Many LEAs have separate 'special' schools organized according to different pathologies and should Gary be removed from Mill House it was likely that he would be sent to a school for children with 'emotional and behavioural difficulties' – the local 'EBD' school. My collusion would probably make inevitable his removal to that school, which would clearly be a punitive response. This 'psychological' assessment was beginning to seem like one of those 'crimes against humanity' of which I had suspected myself earlier (p. 10). I decided to resist.

Gary was quiet with me, and rather than employ specific psychological 'techniques' acquired during training (e.g. Personal Construct Psychology, Brief Therapy) which might make their own particular claims to usefulness in relation to his behaviour (his reported 'difficulties'), I used my power in the situation to suggest that we might do some other work together. I gave Gary as much opportunity to refuse this suggestion as was within my gift but he agreed to perform standardized tests of 'ability' and 'attainment'.[4]

Gary achieved scores of ability which were within what psychometricians would describe as 'the expected range' (roughly between the 15th and 85th centile of a cohort of his age). There was one exception, however, in 'recall of digits'; this is a test of auditory short-term memory which can sometimes indicate the degree of difficulties a child might experience with reading and literacy skills in general. In tests of the 'basic skills' (his 'attainments') Gary scored at the 1st centile in reading, spelling and number with equivalent 'ages' at around the 7-year-old mark. Now Gary was 15 years old and, apart perhaps from some confusions in his working memory, appeared to have abilities which were within the 'expected range'. Despite this discrepancy between his abilities and his attainments, however, I had not been brought in to reassess Gary because of his learning difficulties but because of his behaviour. And Gary is the one who is regarded as an educational failure!

It was Mrs Smith who, during our first meeting, had told me that Gary was 'dyslexic' (I was to forget this remark – a dismissal in itself). Certainly, I have known children with Gary's 'profile' of abilities and attainments who receive diagnoses of 'specific learning difficulties' (dyslexia) and who are then placed in another, different kind of 'special' unit, one which is marked by signs of privilege and exclusivity. Dyslexia was not the reason which had ever been attributed for Gary's school failure, however, as neither Gary nor his family had ever had the opportunities to exert control over their own pathologies.

Gradually, through our joint performance – which appeared to become one of joint interest and commitment – Gary and I seemed to develop our own cautiously playful rhythm. Gary's success in the ability tests might not only have been because he did not know how he should fail, but also perhaps because our intelligences seemed to respond to one another's. Effectively, it seemed as though I was actually using my power and knowledge to say to Gary, '*I am an intelligent person and I know that you are too, so show me*'. He did.

After a while, it was not only the tests which allowed me to see Gary as an intelligent young man, despite being someone who, after ten years of full-time education, still had only a tenuous grasp on those 'basic skills' of reading, writing, spelling and numeracy. In his alert contributions within our conversation Gary told me of his enthusiasms, both for his current schooling and for his future prospects. He told me that he liked this school, that he had made good friends and that he liked particular teachers and subjects. He also told me that he didn't like change.

This 'third' Gary was both interesting and interested and I liked him. Our conversation had been the most enjoyable part of the day and I was glad to have met him.

As we walked back to his class, the conversation continued and Gary told me that it was time for his favourite lesson, art. No surprise there, I suppose, effectively excluded as he was from much of the (literacy-based) curriculum. Pat, the teacher, then not only showed me some of Gary's recent work (pastiche in the style of Van Gogh, GCSE course-work) but s/he also spoke of Gary more positively and with some sensitivity regarding the difficulties which he can present to others in school. I began to experience some hope.

Gary's creativity and potential for learning were to be found not only in his art work, however, for they seemed to be part of who he was, existing as fundamental aspects of his whole personality, even more so perhaps than his propensity to behave badly. For Gary had now shown me his intelligence, his creativity and also his capacity for perfectly reasonable behaviour. How could many of the previous reports, written and verbal, from psychologists and teachers, past and present have missed this 'third' Gary? I might have done so as well but sometimes it can be easier for me to find solace by attributing incompetence to others and thus deny my own intelligences and knowledge of the processes in which I am involved.

Further reflection upon the selection of 'ability' as a measure of Gary, however, can bring into question the abilities of all the professionals with whom he has worked throughout his school career. Blaming others, however, even in order that the pathology could be removed from Gary, would not kill the pathology for it will merely metamorphosize elsewhere, for example, as professional failure.

Gary continued to be wary of me but in another sense I found it reassuring that his ability to mobilize his defences against a figure of authority had not been dulled despite the apparent sincerity of this individual practitioner. Indeed, I argue that it would be vital for Gary to withold his trust, especially since I knew that the social processes which led to our relationship might yet induce my betrayal.

Gary IV – The Lion's Den

The 'fourth' Gary I came to know was mediated by the eyes of another teacher, 'Bernie'.

> *'I cannot attend to the whole class ... he is very demanding ... he has a short concentration span ... he gets frustrated at his reading difficulties. ... I am very concerned at his behaviour. ... I can't trust him alone with the others ... he had a knife ... he encourages the others to misbehave ... he is aggressive in the yard*

> *... he can be menacing ... frightening ... he's clever though, it's always the other people who are at fault.'*

Bernie seemed genuinely disturbed by Gary but these remarks (again taken down as 'field notes' at the time) came somewhat as a surprise, as just a few minutes earlier Gary had spoken warmly to me of this teacher. I had now been at the school for over two hours, however, and I was exhausted.

Bernie went on to tell me of an occasion on which s/he perceived Gary's response to instructions as menacing. During the story, Bernie's bodily, facial and verbal movements became such that I wondered whether such vehemence was a mere reproduction of Gary's menace or whether its contents were filled with other investments. It seemed possible, however, that if Bernie had shown the aggression towards Gary which I was now sensing, that he too, like me, would have felt threatened. One instruction s/he had given to Gary was reproduced for me with such venom that I recoiled, forced to mobilize my own defences still further, averting my eyes, rocking back in my chair to create more physical space between us and concentrating hard to control my breathing.

Gary, however, is a young man who, as many others, will have had reasons to be fearful throughout his life. He has been treated harshly for many years, not only within his organized social environments such as his schools, but also by his stepfather within his home. Gary is someone who, at the age of 6 was regarded as so vulnerable that he was removed from school *'because he had been injured twice by other children'* (early EP report). Gary is also now a 15-year-old boy who, from the age of 8, has been put in schools for children with 'learning difficulties' despite presenting as a *'very bright boy'* (a previous Statement of Special Educational Needs). Gary is also someone who received severe physical punishment delivered over a long period of time by a trusted adult.

I began to wonder how on earth Gary, faced by Bernie's aggression had not either frozen with fear or else lashed out in anger. I was beginning to see Gary's relatively passive responses as either amazingly manipulative (intelligent?) or else little short of heroic. It was time for me to go.

> *'I'll have to come back, Bernie; there are one or two other things I still need to check.'* (Lie)

This was an exit line which could be accessed by my own professional power but, as with the *'coffee'*, it was a possibility within social power relations to which Gary would not have had access. Bernie may well have returned to class either exhausted by the whole experience or else angry at what s/he might perceive as either my impotence or else my incompetence. Enough. I must go.

> *'How did you get on?'*

Oh no! I had finally just been about to sneak out of the school when another teacher stopped me in my tracks.

'Charming isn't he?'

If only I could reply as I wanted in response to the tone! What right had this new teacher to speak of Gary with such dismissive sarcasm. Before I was to be granted a safe passage from that place, however, I was expected to provide a correct answer to the question which took the appearance of the only *real* question inside the whole process of 'psychological assessment' and which was now being asked of me again, in between the lines.

The moment of betrayal was at hand.

So I ran ...

'He's done really well this morning.'

So s/he chased ...

'he shouldn't be here though.'

So I turned and parried ...

'he's a bright lad isn't he?'

So s/he struck ...

'yes, he's too bright for us.'

Sorry Gary. ... I should have seen it coming ... perhaps my resistance can be of little use to you if other, powerful professionals are too deeply committed to the pathology.

Gary V – Seeing Someone New

By the end of this particular session I had decided to offer my availability sometimes for Gary and his mother (was this guilt?) so in response to a remark of his that he had *'other drawings at home'* I asked if I might visit him there to have another chat with them both.

On arrival, Mrs Smith provided further evidence to support my view that, if Gary could not be removed from school through the statementing process (this often acts as an unofficial exclusion process) then he would be removed anyway through the official exclusion procedures. All three of us seemed to share this understanding, for this was yet another knowledge not restricted to a psychological expertise. The professional search for any signs of failure on Gary's part and also the refusal to acknowledge any of his efforts or successes seemed relentless and eventually, the decision seemed to emerge between us that perhaps the situation at Mill House was untenable.

Now whilst we had been considering methods of resistance which would have enabled Gary to stay at Mill House, the reader might feel that it would have been in

Gary's best interest all along for him to have found another school. On what basis, though, should Gary be removed from Mill House and suffer exclusion again? Certainly not on his own evidence. For not only did Gary say that he wanted to remain there (he had told me of the subjects and the various teachers and friends whom he liked) but he told me explicitly that he didn't want another move, because he doesn't like change and finds *'new things difficult'*.

Mrs Smith too had not wanted Gary to be exposed to the failure which would almost inevitably await him now, either in the guise of a mainstream curriculum or else in the guise of a more punitive establishment. She also felt that Gary would be 'safer' at Mill House. These were the reasons to resist Gary's removal and such reasons are often used in order to sustain the exclusion but the change of school now would merely replicate the conditions of his original exclusions years ago, other exclusions which the family had not sought. Those earlier exclusions too had been perpetrated in a dynamic enterprise within the education system which mobilized against Gary and his mother. In my view, that enterprise was still hard at work in their lives.

Mrs Smith and Gary were again to be denied access to those very qualities of which, it could be argued, they seemed to be most in need; some degree of stability, dignity, respect and perhaps social integration. At the very moment when Gary needed such help (the potential benefits of which were actually being recognized by the legal structures of 'Formal Assessment') it looked likely that more punitive measures were to be called upon which would be able to drive home with even greater force the effects of the family's personal tragedies and social pathologies.

I continued to be amazed by the family's stoicism and resilience in a situation which may well have defeated others, including myself, and also perhaps many of the other professionals by whom they were currently being judged. I had to keep a check on my increasing tendency to see them both as victims, however, for although this was perhaps a position preferable to their situation as offenders, not only was it patronising in the extreme but it would also suggest a view of my own position as heroic rescuer. A beckoning danger here is that we can move further towards analyses which see the various participants, Gary, his mother, his teachers and myself variously as individual oppressors, victims and saviours and therefore lose sight of the *processes*, the movements, of pathologization in which we are all involved.

As I left the house that evening, Gary showed me to the door and, looking back, I was amazed by what I saw. For as I turned I saw yet another Gary, a Gary who now took a very different form. It was at this moment that, for the first time, I seemed to see that Gary was not the same as his previously attributed pathologies. It was only now, through my eyes' new-found capacity to separate Gary from his pathologies that I could realize that my previous efforts to resist the pathologizing tendency had hitherto been unsuccessful. Despite my resistances, and no matter what form they had taken, until that moment Gary and his pathologies had remained inseparable in my eyes. Just for a moment I was able to see a new Gary.

The Decision ...

The LEA decided that Gary should stay at Mill House. Perhaps the further acts of collaborative resistance over the ensuing month conducted together with Mrs Smith and Gary had had an effect. Mrs Smith told me that school staff were now all working really well with him and were attempting to address positively his educational needs which, she had maintained all along, were connected principally to his 'dyslexia' and to his inability to work at the level of which he could be capable.

Mrs Smith was also able to tell me that Gary had been attending for counselling on a regular basis for several weeks now but whilst his behaviour had begun to stabilize inside school, she hinted that his behaviour in the home was presenting her with more difficulties. Now that some of Gary's needs were being addressed in school, however, Mrs Smith felt more able to consider her own needs and she took the initiative of asking me for help regarding the difficulties she had experienced over the years. Mrs Smith again acted upon advice and she joined a group for parents of children who 'survived abuse' run by social services.

I was beginning to think that the resistance had been worthwhile after all so I then visited Gary and his mother for one last time in order to discuss the possibility of their inclusion in my research. Mrs Smith met me at the door with nasty marks to her face.

'If you're wondering what the bruises are I bumped into a lamp-post.'

Endpiece

Now it may be that in reading my descriptions of Gary that you have found yourself apportioning blame in the various situations which arose. Possibly, attention as reader may have been drawn to the accounts of the teachers, administrators or psychologists – all committed professionals. Perhaps attention might have been drawn to Gary's supposedly innate characteristics, those of his mother or step-father. Certainly, there were many participants in what was a very real drama.

Blame, however, may too easily be allocated at an individual level, especially when the extents of professional activity can seem so variable. To what extent, however, are individuals responsible for the outcomes of their endeavours when the situations seem to set limits upon their field of agency and thus limit the range of options available for their consideration. For indeed, it can seem in certain circumstances that some outcomes, for example Gary's placement in a mainstream school, actually become unthinkable.

This chapter developed around a case study taken from my professional practice. The important themes introduced here and explored during the book include:

* critical examination of professional practices and relationships;
* the embedding of exclusionary processes within professional practices;
* the existence of power relations within professional practices with children;
* that professional practices can resist exclusion and pathologization;
* that pathologies/blame can be mobile, shifting from one individual/category to another e.g. from a child to a teacher or psychologist;
* that individual professional acts occur within collective, social practices and thus pose ethical and moral questions at the boundaries of responsibility;

- the minutiae of everyday events can be imbued with many meanings and matters of importance;
- meaning and knowledge are not restricted to the concrete life of words;
- the unsatisfactory nature of prevailing models of intelligence and ability.

Suggestions for Further Reading

Ideological Dilemmas (Billig et al., 1988) explores the complexities and dilemmatic nature of things which can confront us within seemingly simple activities and practices.

Foucault's (1977) *Discipline and Punish* is a relatively straightforward account of the emergence of public institutions and the growth of specific professional practices during the last three hundred years.

Wendy Hollway's (1989) *Subjectivity and Method in Psychology* deals with experimental methodology and provides useful pointers in qualitative research, not least in respect of the role of the experimenters themselves.

3   Pathologizing Children
Power and Regulation

That element of tragedy which lies in the very heart of frequency, has not yet wrought itself into the coarse emotion of mankind, and perhaps our frames could hardly bear much of it. If we had a keen vision and feeling of all ordinary human life it would be like hearing the grass grow and the squirrel's heart beat, and we should die of that roar which lies on the other side of silence. As it is, the quickest of us walk about well wadded with stupidity.

(Eliot [1871–2], 1996)

This chapter engages with the origins and development of child psychopathology. It locates the professional practices associated with psychopathologization within economic and social spheres and charts their relationship with the emergence of complex forms of government during the last three hundred years or so. The chapter thus provides an historicized account of the ways in which professionals continue to devise new technologies which map shifting constructions of abnormality and thus contribute to the industrialization of human differences.

Labels for Children

As the 'science of the nature, function, and phenomena, of human mind' (Concise Oxford Dictionary, 7th Edition), the project of psychology would seem to be well placed to promote and develop in its practitioners George Eliot's understanding of a 'keen vision and feeling of all human life'. Well, in Gary's case, the practices and discourses which permeate child psychology in education were sufficient to suggest (or indeed confirm in the view of the legislative authority) that he had both 'behavioural difficulties' and 'learning difficulties'. These seem to be meagre achievements, however, for as mere descriptions they appear to say very little about Gary. And yet, in certain domains of activity and endeavour – for example, 'special educational needs' – many (adult) professionals ascribe such labels to thousands of children in Britain each year,[1] often with huge effects upon the lives of the children and upon also the lives of all the adults who are involved.

What, then, might be the nature of the 'roar' which lies on the other side of Gary's 'behavioural' and 'learning' difficulties? I argue that we would hear at least some of the noise were we to shift from Gary's individualized 'difficulties' to the processes which generate the (search for) psychopathologies in the first place. For I argue here that it is the processes which simultaneously create and demand psychopathologies and which encourage assaults on children (like Gary) which, too often, evade the gaze of analysis.

Whilst pathology can be defined as the science of bodily diseases, which is related to Medicine, psychopathology is a term for those practices which, organized broadly within the domain of Psychology, have flourished in a search for diseases of the mind. It is through the expansion of such processes, however, that children can be allocated, not merely a label (for example, of either behavioural or learning difficulties) but also a plethora of associated discourses and practices which circulate in the social domain. I argue that the meanings and outcomes organized around categories can be far from benign and that they can carry with them the stigmatizing effect of a social disease. I also argue here, therefore, that the allocation of an individualized psychopathology can constitute an attack on a child, as a stigma which can have lasting social and also economic consequences for the child recipient.

Now at one level, a child's 'behavioural difficulties' or 'learning difficulties' might seem very mild in comparison with the more dangerous connotations of adult psychopathology, for example, 'psychopath' or 'schizophrenic'. But while the more distinctly adult psychopathologies are the province of psychiatry, and 'difficulties' in learning and behaviour are usually the subject of practices within education and child psychology, the power of the latter terms can be detected nonetheless in the very material consequences of their application. For example, in Gary's case diagnoses of difficulties in 'learning' and 'behaviour' had led to:

- several changes of school;
- possible restriction of future economic opportunities;
- analyses in which the circumstances and experiences of his social relations can fade from view;
- the reduction of all other aspects of his personality;
- the lack of a vigorous search for his potentials.

In this chapter, therefore, I look to create a means of challenging those individualized representations of both Gary and his teachers in Chapter 2 by considering the institutional, governmental and, not least, the historical processes which are implicated in the (social) pathologization of children generally and which, I argue, will have been active in the pathologization of Gary. In order to consider the ways in which both the events and the individual lives represented in Chapter 2 might be contextualized, I draw here upon a range of analyses which can be found at source in the works of Foucault, Rose and Parker and also in previous work (Billington, 1996).

Government, Knowledge and Power

The ways in which people in Western countries have gradually become subject to complex forms of 'governmentality' during the last three hundred years have been charted in some detail by, amongst others, Nikolas Rose (1989) and, previously, Michel Foucault (1977).

> 'Governmentality' is the totality of the very particular ways in which the supervision of populations has developed beyond national governments, permeating an array of institutions and practices. Governmentality has been described by Foucault as, 'the ensemble formed by institutions, procedures, analyses and reflections, the calculations and tactics, that allow the exercise of this very specific albeit complex form of power, which has as its target population' (Foucault, 1979).

A particular contribution made by both Foucault and Rose is that they placed the theories and practices of child psychology and education upon a larger map of world history and in so doing created an important vantage point from which to view contemporary claims to knowledge. In this chapter, therefore, I begin to place knowledge about children and their psychopathology within a history of the last three hundred years during which Western societies have become structured in unique ways i.e. nation states organized according to the demands of a capitalized economy.

During the last three hundred years there would appear to have developed a positive correlation between the rate of expansion of these economies and the complexity of the forms of governmentality which have ensued. The institutional practices which have arisen have not only offered the possibility of greater control of the population but they have encouraged both the proliferation of new forms of population and identity, together with, at the same time, the creation of resistances which themselves have the capacity to fuel further expansion. Indeed, Foucault saw the practices of governmentality develop as social power relations, and suggested that in order to continue and consolidate its expansion governmentality would necessitate capacities not only to regulate populations but also capacities to resist that regulation.

Here, therefore, I suggest that it is children who (following other populations) have now become one of the principal populations which have been targeted by many of the above forms of governmentality. The result, from the nineteenth century onwards, has been a huge growth in the children industry (of which this book is a part), and this growth has continued apace since the Second World War, with armies of professionals providing 'expert' knowledge about the 'true' 'nature' of children. Indeed, it can be argued that this growth has been such that children have become the most 'intensively governed sector of personal existence' (Rose, 1989, p. 121).

Continuing this theme, it can be argued that individual 'technologies of government'[2] such as those developed by experts within the domains of developmental, child or educational psychology (see Burman, 1994), together with specific parliamentary legislation such as the 1993 and 1996 Education Acts, have constantly formed and re-formed in order to adjust both the contemporary concept of childhood and

23

the material circumstances of children. Such governmental partnerships are rarely harmonized in ways which afford simple analysis (see Riley, 1983) but one example might be the ways in which psychologized theories of child development have coursed through the veins of family policy and legislation enacted by the British government during, and immediately following the Second World War, for example in Education and Health.

Increasingly, children and childhood seem to have become subjected to a particular kind of scrutiny, one which is affected by the social, cultural and material circumstances in which children exist. Childhood itself has developed as a discrete population which can be subject to change, thus according with the properties of contemporary forms of governmentality. That the family and, in particular, children should have been the focus of so much governmental energy and mounting public anxiety is manifest, therefore, both in the continuing expansion of child legislation, for example, the 1989 Children Act, together with innumerable Education Acts, but also in the expansion of the children industry into the media which continues to generate discussions and advice for parents and carers.

This focus of governmentality upon the lives of children has sought to challenge what is feared to be the spontaneous animalism or potential for unreason within human beings, forces which, we are now encouraged to believe, are at their most pure, least controllable and most potent during childhood. It is through the definition and regulation of this supposed unreason within children that we can also identify childhood as one of the categories of resistance against a regulation which seeks to impose itself in the name of reason. This struggle has been recognized as one of the foundations of contemporary Western psychology, 'a moment would come when, from this animality of madness, would be deduced the idea of a mechanistic psychology' (Foucault, 1967, p. 76).

Labels for Government

Psychologized discourses circulating within the system of education have made important contributions as acts of government which, for example, with increasing tenacity, enable the identification and pathologization of children whose very being is considered unreasonable: children who are allocated a social disability in whatever form, physical, mental or emotional. It is through the discourses which permeate institutions such as Education, Health and Social Services that attacks can be organized against children's resistance to the power of reason, government and responsibility, both at a structural and at an individual level. Such institutions validate the allocation of pathologies as part of the processes of governmentality by recourse to a very specific kind of science – 'scientific discourses which render knowable the normal and pathological functioning of humans' (Rose, 1989, p. ix). It is knowledge that is at stake here, therefore, for knowledge is essential to different forms of governmentality, 'the production, circulation, organization and authorization of truths that incarnate what is to be governed, which make it thinkable, calculable and practicable' (Rose, 1989, p. 6).

It is science which has undertaken to authorize such truths but it is only particular kinds of scientific practice which have been assigned the power to become synonymous with 'fact, truth and reason' (Williams, 1976). The particular kinds of scientific practice which have been applied to the burgeoning studies of human 'nature' since the nineteenth century have often been based upon methods which had originally been applied successfully in studies of the physical world. That such methods can necessarily provide all knowledge of the human world is an illusion, however, for in the social world 'our science is not knowledge ... it can achieve neither truth nor probability' (Tolman, 1994, p. 28). Such scientific methods, however, can if looked for, provide us with knowledge; not necessarily knowledge of children but knowledge of the power relations in which they live their lives.

> The regime of disciplinary power ... differentiates individuals from one another ... measures in quantitative terms of value the abilities, the level, the 'nature' of individuals ... it traces the limit that will define difference in relation to all other differences, the external frontier of the abnormal.
>
> (Foucault, 1979, pp. 182–183)

Practising Pathologization With Children: Scientific Discourses Within Psychology and Education

The intense focus upon children, their development, their abilities and behaviours, has permeated the social fabric to bring governmentality and (disciplinary) power relations to all children at an individual level. Rather than investigating further individual children like Gary, however, of interest here are the ways in which particular scientific practices have been organized to make specific contributions to this enterprise, for example by identifying and, if necessary, removing children from certain social arenas such as school.

It is by focusing at a day-to-day level upon individual children rather than the practices themselves that practitioners have concealed not only the processes in which many hypotheses were first generated but often the innately social character of the processes themselves; for it is within social processes and power relations that any hypotheses are generated. Whilst they offer opportunities for both regulation and resistance, however, they have developed in order to serve the interests, not necessarily of science, but of those whose power allows them to make claims to 'fact, truth and reason'. It is not always the quest for fact and truth which determines scientific practices, therefore, but the ownership of reason and its partnership with economic powers and governmentality. In such practices, science slips silently away.

Perhaps Gary and his mother might have chosen different forms of professional intervention, but in seeking truths about him, the scientific practices had been organized by institutions to investigate certain characteristics or differences deemed unacceptable – his 'difficulties'. This search was to be conducted by various professionals such as teachers, social workers, psychologists and administrators, each having a particular contribution to make within the process. The nature of their respective areas of expertise will be touched upon later in the chapter but I will first address the principles and scientific discourses upon which professional practices are based for, I argue, it is the same principles and discourses which tend to pervade all the practices of those who work with children.

Rank

Once again, recourse to history permits us to consider theories and practices which many child professionals continue to use but which many will probably no longer see:

> In the eighteenth century, 'rank' begins to define the great form of individuals in the educational order: rows or ranks of pupils in the class, corridors, courtyards; rank attributed to each pupil at the end of each task and each examination; the rank obtains from week to week, month to month, year to year; an alignment of age groups, one after another; a succession of subjects taught and questions treated, according to an order of increasing difficulty.
>
> (Foucault, 1977, pp. 146–147)

Foucault allows us to see that whilst 'rank' today acts as a fundamental means of organizing children's lives, so completely has it become immersed within our culture, and so effectively have our professionals been trained in its application that we have to strive now to question its relevance or recognize even its presence. An historical account, however, can remind us that there was a time when adult practices based on 'rank' were only just emerging. As such we can conceive of a time when rank would not have affected the lives of children in the same way, thus allowing us to reflect, therefore, upon our contemporary professional work.

The importance of articulating the origins of such a simple principle is that the use of rank has become one of the building blocks upon which the whole system of child surveillance continues to be built. Developmental and child psychology too has been built upon a fundamental tendency to rank children, and indeed it generates technologies which enable such practices, for example, to rank children according to their 'abilities'. A Foucauldian or historical account can allow us to see that whilst such practices claim an a priori knowledge regarding individual children they are but transient social activities belonging to a particular historical and cultural context.

Measurement

In order to rank children, we need first to measure them in some way and in Western social science this has been achieved by stat(e)istics ('the science of state', Rose, 1989). The measurement of children, their learning or behaviour, is a core activity for many who work with children. In particular, it is a core activity for teachers and also for psychologists who work with children or within the Education system, and it is an activity which is inculcated in professional training courses. Measurement helps to control the complexity of government for it is through measurement that children's lives can be reduced to the smallest number of characteristics in the shortest time available. Indeed, the measurement of children can operate in ways which deny individuals any identity whatsoever.

The psychometric test has long been the main weapon in the psychologist's armoury and its value lies in its promise to reduce any individual to a single figure. The tests are thus an effective weapon in the battery of assessment techniques which are used to regulate and pathologize children's 'learning difficulties' and which can be used subsequently to place them against other children according to rank. However, Foucauldian accounts of regulation are complex and these very techniques which are used to regulate children may also contain within them the seeds of resistance.

Categorization

Indeed, it was this resistance which I invoked in Gary's case for, having been referred to me because of his 'behavioural difficulties', I used psychometric tests to resist such a simplistic pathologization. It could be argued that this was a successful ploy, for Gary achieved test scores which suggested that, whilst he was of 'average intelligence', his attainment scores in literacy and numeracy were very low and were, therefore, not commensurate. This discrepancy between his abilities and his attainments in basic skills was of statistical significance and I therefore used my professional power to deflect attention away from his pathology of 'behavioural difficulties' and chose instead for Gary a categorization of 'specific learning difficulties' (dyslexia) which I predicted would lead to less punitive social consequences. It is possible, therefore, to employ those technologies of regulation and measurement in order to resist a pathology, but here it was achieved only by invoking the powers of science and reason and indeed only by selecting instead another categorization.

Now, once again, I argue that such categories are devised according to a knowledge which is far from being 'a priori' and that current professional categorizations of children are historically and culturally specific and, therefore, subject to constant change and revision. This is a position which is adopted by a critical psychology (see Tolman and Maiers, 1991), and it is a political position which opposes many current practices which separate and exclude individual children by trapping them within pathologized sub-groups.

This whole enterprise of measuring, ranking and categorizing children has consumed much human energy within the domains of psychology and education but as industrial, social activity it invokes the questions and discourses of 'normality' and 'abnormality' which have preoccupied institutions and indeed the development of social sciences generally in Western societies during the last two hundred years.

The Progress of Abnormality

Increasingly, psychologists have undertaken to provide the science, or rather technologies, to support this irrational desire which lurks within Western forms of reason – which is the eradication of unreason itself (see Walkerdine, 1988) – through the creation of the ultimate normal human being. Once again, statistics has offered itself as an efficient tool of social regulation and the normal distribution curve has simultaneously provided opportunities not only to hide individual identities but also to contain potentials and capacities for unreason: 'The capacity of any individual could be established in terms of their location along that curve; the intellect reduced to order. ... Binet transformed it from a technique for diagnosing the pathological into a device for creating a hierarchy of the normal' (Rose, 1989, pp. 138–139).

The axis of 'normal/abnormal' provides an important site for governmentality and the associated discourses which have arisen have infiltrated, not only the more usual forms of governmental practices, Education, Health, Social Work, but have also gained new life by operating within a more recent and vigorous arena for social discourses, for the media constitutes perhaps the newest site of governmentality. Psychopathology, therefore, is linked to a social quest for the 'normal' in order that unreason, in the form of anonymized populations, can be controlled, regulated and made subject to economic and political powers.

The quest for diseases of the mind had its origins in social practices which had proved successful in the search for diseases of the body. Whilst the practice of confining diseased populations has a long history (see Foucault, 1967), it was during the sixteenth and seventeenth centuries, however, that the use of specific places of confinement (for example the leper colonies which could be found outside many European cities) was extended. This expansion of the places of confinement occurred initially in order to hold the increasing numbers of both expendable and migratory populations who provided the growing market economies with a cheap and flexible source of cheap labour. Gradually, the colonies of the physically diseased were supplemented by these new colonies for the socially diseased, and the technologies of confinement which were trialled in the new prisons and hospitals of the eighteenth century were further extended in order that populations of poor people, for example, could be confined in the new workhouses.

The similarities between the ways in which were born the workhouses, the modern hospital and prison, and the characteristics of the social practices therein are difficult to ignore. Whilst these institutions came to house all those who could not always contribute actively to economic expansion, the new institutions themselves provided sites for the expansion of other forms of economic activity and encouraged the development of new methods of social control, for example through overt forms of policing and, less obviously, medicine. In time, the principles of social confinement which underpinned these new institutional forms were further extended to other populations who were perhaps neither criminal, sick nor necessarily unemployable. The asylum was thus born for all those others who could not conform to eighteenth-century notions of reason and who could be classified as mad or insane.

Whilst the hospitalization of the physically diseased provided a convenient, contained site for the expansion of the new medical activities, it was natural that such practices were extended also to the asylum and here we see the further expansion of medical activities into diseases of the mind. To conclude that hospitals and asylums became places for enlightened scientific pursuit would be erroneous, however, for in both sites there was often more 'governmentality' than 'science', 'It is thought that Tuke and Pinel opened the asylum to medical knowledge. They did not introduce science, but a personality, whose powers borrowed from science only their disguise, or at most their justification' (Foucault, 1967, p. 271).

In summary, therefore, during the seventeenth and eighteenth centuries, large populations began to be identified as 'abnormal', categorized as either the physically sick, the unemployed, the criminal or the mad. Increasingly, all people became subject to the possibilities offered by the new phenomenon of mass social confinement, for example, which all relate to particular forms of industrialized work.

During the second half of the nineteenth century these processes were extended to the lives of children through, for example, legislation in child employment and education (e.g. 1870 Education Act and the beginnings of a mass education system).

Confining Children: Power, Knowledge, Expertise

Now for those of us who work in the 'caring' professions, recourse to Foucauldian accounts of history can make uncomfortable reading. Many of us will have chosen such professions, no doubt, for the best of motives, for example, perhaps a willingness to help those less fortunate than ourselves, through genuine human kindness or else generosity of spirit. To Foucault, however, these are the resistances which are made available within contemporary social power relations and the possibilities for which will continue to present themselves.

Training for professionals who work with children, whilst acknowledging the liberal discourses of help and care (resistances), can too often inculcate its novitiates more thoroughly in regulatory practices, for how else could the processes of social exclusion and confinement continue to operate and expand so effectively? It is my intention here to concentrate on two particular domains of social activity which emerged in the latter half of the nineteenth century and which have provided the institutional sites through which governmentality has been extended to the lives of children.

Education and psychology have both developed as 'enclosures of knowledge' (see Rose and Miller, 1992) during the last one hundred and fifty years. Such 'enclosures' are again subject to social power relations developing in part, because 'discipline sometimes requires enclosure, the specification of a place heterogenous to all others and closed in upon itself' (Foucault, 1977, p. 141). Both of these enclosures have developed the properties of regimes of 'licensure ... [which] empower certain bodies to act in a certain professional capacity, both legitimizing and regulating at the same time' (Rose, 1989, p. 190).

In order to operate effectively, both education and psychology have encouraged the development of the notion of the 'expert'. Both these enclosures are filled now with experts who are paid for particular forms of knowledge, supposedly based on scientific information about children which is often presented in the form of tables, measurements and categorizations. Too often, however, the knowledge is based, not on science but on the power vested in the position of the expert to lay claim not merely to science, but to fact, truth and reason. In performing their science, the expert is often allowed to escape individual scrutiny as they too are required to lose their individual identity within the social power relations: 'The personage of the expert, embodying neutrality, authority and skill in a wise figure, operating according to an ethical code "beyond good and evil" ' (Rose and Miller, 1992, p. 187).

Schools: Locations for Revolution or Confinement?

In the early part of the nineteenth century educating the masses was considered to be a dangerous proposition which would de-stabilize the social order by encouraging a kind of learning and (political) knowledge which could serve to foment revolution. By the end of the century, however, schools had developed, not as breeding grounds for revolutionary activities or social unrest but, on the contrary, schools proved themselves capable of establishing the principles of order and reason and also as institutions in which social training and governmentality could take precedence over learning.

Whilst literacy and numeracy provided the overt curriculum, and indeed such skills were being demanded increasingly by a commerce and industry desirous of improving economic competitiveness, a vital part of the curriculum lay hidden in the rules and often unspoken protocols of the social behaviour demanded within schools. The authority of the teacher to demand attention and order, the controls over the timing and manner of speaking, and the regulation of individual movements within school formed the hidden curriculum which was to extend and impose upon children the disciplinary power which had recently applied to adults. As an institution, therefore, education supported the principles of Western reason and governmentality and as such adopted the role of a 'semi-judicial structure' (Foucault, 1967, p. 40), concerned with social order as much as with learning.

From the outset, however, some children proved not to be amenable to such training and control and they would be removed from the educational arena. Medicine seized the market opportunity as many children were excluded from the education system on account of, effectively, either physical or mental handicap diagnosed by the authority of a medical expert. The pathologization and subsequent exclusion of children was thus woven into the very formation of mass education in partnership with medicine and technology.

Whilst administering categories could be simple, however, the numbers involved were large and 'experts' in children with opinions about the 'nature' of the human mind began to emanate from the new psychology, offering means of regulating the population at a reduced cost: 'something significant occurred in a period from about 1875 to about 1925 ... the formation of psychology as a coherent and individuated scientific discourse' (Rose, 1985, p. 3).

Psychology not only began to encourage the adoption of the scientific methods which were employed in medicine but supported the principles of diagnosis and pathology with a statistical armoury of 'rank', 'measurement' and new approaches towards human 'categorization'. Psychology began to claim authority over the pathology of human mind and behaviour. This account of the expansion of psychology can be misleading, however, for it does not explain sufficiently either the complexity or the social absorption of the emerging practices.

> The scientific discourse of individual psychology did not form in a pure space of knowledge, but neither was it called into existence through the force of social exigencies. It was made possible by other ways of thinking of the nature, origin and treatment of mental pathology, and by certain conceptions of the role and objectives of good government and the laws of economic and social life.
>
> (Rose, 1985, p. 7)

Both psychology and education, therefore, formed as sites for social and political activity which, through their application to children, could contribute to the processes of governmentality by creating stories of the normal and abnormal child.

The stories of children which were devised could be justified by scientific discourses whose methods and practices were characterized, not necessarily by scientific truths, but rather by the power invested in their claims to such truths.

'The language of abnormal psychology is enmeshed within institutions of mental diagnosis and surveillance' (Parker, 1996, p. 4) and indeed, the professional activities which characterize both the institutional domains of psychology and education are observation and examination. In the case of Gary, whilst other people's stories contributed to my assessment, I only had two primary sources of information. Firstly, there were the observations of Gary in the schoolyard and in the classroom and secondly, there was the individual testing.

Now a legacy of the scientific methods which had been tried and tested in the physical sciences is that the experimenter should be objective. In the human sciences, however, such a demand is barely credible, for what is the experimenter/tester of humans other than another human. Surely, a fundamental premise for social sciences is that both experimenter/tester and the test subject are in relation-to one another, whether or not both parties are able to view the relationship. I argue that any experiment, study or research in the social sciences involves human relationships which will themselves co-exist in the web of power relations.

The exclusive application of linear, hypothesis forming and testing models of psychological practices can conjure the illusion that the psychologist might become invisible; the observed subject has no such choice to make. The modern psychologist, for example, in disassociating themselves from the observed is participating in a potentially sinister and unscientific social sleight-of-hand which is in itself evidence of the existing power relations. My observation of Gary in the schoolyard is one such example, for it was I who had the power to have 'eyes that see without being seen' (Foucault, 1977, p. 171).

Both observation and examination, whether undertaken by psychologists or any other professional working with children, are part of the web of power relations and have proved to be successful weapons within the armoury of governmentality and surveillance. In choosing to change the representation of Gary's pathology from behaviour difficulties to specific learning difficulties, I did not alter the power relationships but I can claim to have used the power of my position to resist the more punitive effects to which he would otherwise have become subject. Gary had no such choice.

Endpiece

That people have suffered confinement throughout history is not at issue. Unique, however, is the growth during the last three hundred years of a whole culture in which disciplinary power has been able to infiltrate both body and mind through complex forms of pathology and governmentality. Too often, 'science' (or rather technology) has provided a safe but unscientific refuge for the emissaries of discipline – 'the minor civil servants of moral orthopaedics ... doctors, chaplains, psychiatrists, psychologists, educationalists' (Foucault, 1977, pp. 10–11).

The analyses in this chapter, based as they are upon historicized accounts of pathology, power and government, the model for which was provided by Foucault and Rose, may themselves seem unduly harsh and punitive. A more benign account, however, would leave the regulatory powers unscathed and allow us to retreat to the warmth, security and generous benevolence of our professional positions.

Meanwhile, many children are called to account for their difficulties throughout their childhood and for some like Gary, the wounds may never heal. The totality of the processes which can be located in the site of special educational needs constitutes a child psychopathology which permits the following outcomes:

- a psychopathology can result in a child being excluded from their existing social relations (e.g. a child might be required to change schools);
- a psychopathology can thus separate a child from future social possibilities and opportunities (e.g. a child's future economic and employment chances might be restricted);
- the allocation of a psychopathology to a child serves to represent them as separate from the processes of their social relations (e.g. it separates the individual child from the environmental circumstances and contexts in which they operate);
- a psychopathology represents as separate, individual characteristics which cannot possibly exist outside a child's own complex system of unities (e.g. the allocation of terms such as Asperger's Syndrome as a primary means of social identification can separate certain qualities from the other, unique aspects of their personality);
- a psychopathology can act to separate a child from their abilities and intelligences (e.g. by failing to identify possibilities, either inside or outside reductionist defintions such as 'behavioural difficulties' or 'autism').

Suggestions for Further Reading

Michel Foucault's *Madness and Civilization* (1967) and once again, *Discipline and Punish* (1977) are books worth reading for their contextualizations of contemporary domains of Psychology and Education within a world history.

Nikolas Rose's *Governing the Soul* (1989) examines more closely the shaping of modern Psychology by its willingness to accede to economic and governmental demands.

Deconstructing Developmental Psychology (Burman, 1994) poses critical challenges to the preferred stories of children which underpin traditional developmental psychology.

Deconstructing Psychopathology (Parker et al., 1995) considers further different forms of psychopathologization in a number of contemporary contexts.

4 Speaking of Mary

It is my habit to give an account to myself of the characters I meet with: can I give any true account of my own?

(Eliot [1879], 1995, p. 3)

How do we speak about children? How do we speak with them? Do the answers to these questions affect our work with them? This chapter concerns language and in particular the nature of spoken language. Some theories about language are explored briefly, for example, its communicative, expressive or material nature, and are applied to my work with children in educational contexts. The reader is also asked to consider whether there exist elements of language which lie beyond the words themselves. The chapter is organized into two main parts. In the first part – Language and Objectivity – the reader is invited to consider some common realist assumptions made about professional accounts of children. In the second part, however – Language and Beyond – the reader is confronted with interpretive approaches and theories of language which implicate elements which lie outside the life of the words themselves. As in the case of Gary, the various forms of written evidence are selected from my own 'field notes' taken at the time, extracts from my reports (Psychological Advice to the Local Education Authority under the 1993 Education Act), extracts from children's 'Statements' made by the Local Education Authority, and extracts from reports written by other professionals.

Introduction

In both Chapters 4 and 5, readers are introduced again to representations of children with whom I have worked, Mary and James. In this chapter, however, arguments are explored concerning aspects of spoken language and narrative through which representations of children are made. For, whether as teacher, social worker, health professional or psychologist, our professional trades are largely dependent on the exchange of language. I argue, however, that professionals working with children may often miss some of the complexity and variability of their own language use and as such psychologists (in my case) can be accused of being non-scientific.

Language use contains within its movements many individual separations and possibilities for exclusion. The key issues include:

- the historical significance of the change from largely oral-based cultures to ones which are based on literacy; it is easy to overlook the significance of the subsequent birth of a mass education system and its attendant drive for universal literacy, processes which are, in practical terms, still only about a hundred years old (NB historically, the Education Acts of 1870 and 1944 are of particular significance);
- the transitions in children from pre-linguistic to oral speech and from oral speech to literacy; developmentally, those moments when a child's cries and babbles gradually begin to take the forms and shapes of words and, later, realizations that words and sounds can have visual, symbolic lives are both crucial to a child's experiences of education;
- thirdly, the life of the extra-linguistic; what might lie beyond words? Separations are considered, those which can occur between the words spoken and the speaker, the words written and the writer, the words written and the person written about, in this chapter, Mary or James.

Historicized accounts will again support theoretical concerns and as such reference will be made to Vygotskian, psychoanalytic and discourse analytic readings, all of which attempt to conceive of representations of the past.

In expressing my concern about the implicit claims to accuracy made in professional stories about children I provide examples of the ways in which (psychologists') words can be purloined as acts of government. I consider too the ways in which (written) reports can be used by institutions as justification for committing acts of separation and exclusion upon children and their parents. I argue also that in the process of compiling a 'Statement of Special Educational Needs' for a child the professionals too may well be separated from the vitality of their own acts of speaking and writing.

I suggest, therefore, three theoretical/practical aspects of language:

- language can be considered expressive; the words we use can be a sophisticated representation of feelings we are experiencing and can be uttered, therefore, primarily for our own benefit (see Bion, 1962, for theoretical elaboration);
- language can be communicative; the words we use can attempt to explain particular ideas or feelings to someone else, or else be used in response to ideas and feelings expressed by others (see Vygotsky, 1986, for further consideration);
- language can be material; this is a realist argument which suggests that the words we use are as matter, moving in-relation-to other objects through space and time (see Lacan, 1977).

The ways in which language is any of these, however, expressive, communicative or material, may not necessarily become known, either to the speaker, to the listener or to the reader. Therefore, should accuracy be claimed by a language user who purports to speak or write of the truth of another, it is the claimant and their reasons for claiming truth and accuracy which could become a focus for a more scientific investigation.

Once again, I consider the processes and outcomes of separating and excluding children by resisting here the total separation of theory and practice. The reader will, therefore, be asked again to tolerate, not only the intertwining of theory and practice, but also different ways of representing children. In particular, the reader is invited to consider claims to 'truth' made through language and to consider the need for a theorization of professional accounts of children. Indeed, the question which George Eliot's character Theophrastus Such poses at the beginning of the chapter should not be regarded as being of merely literary or philosophical significance, for it accords with the nature of practical scientific inquiry as proposed in this book.

In this chapter, therefore, I argue for analyses which are sensitive to the complexities of narrative, language and text in order that claims to truth and reality in professional texts can be examined more closely. The analyses of texts in themselves might then lead to an understanding of the productive processes involved in their creation. At the same time, such analyses might lead to the recognition and employment of conceptual frameworks which facilitate more truly scientific observations and interpretations than can currently be the case.

LANGUAGE AND OBJECTIVITY

As child professionals, we use words all the time to describe or represent the children with whom we work. To what extent, however, do those words we use speak for themselves?

One facet of analytical concern here is the importance of the concepts and beliefs which lie inside the lives of the words used by individual (professional) participants. The value in adopting discourse analytic (for example, Burman and Parker, 1993; Billington, 1995) approaches is their concern not just for words but for meaning too, as opposed to the person's mind or behaviour of whom the words are written. Such approaches are necessary, for professional accounts in particular often seem to detach from their creators and at times, in a striving to focus upon the 'other' (e.g. the child), they almost seem intent on denying the conceptual life of the author. Analytically, however, such a position seems tenuous in the extreme, for 'perceivers without concepts, as Kant almost said, are blind' (MacIntyre, 1981, p. 79) and also, 'the old view of the disinterested researcher is almost wholly out of date' (Young, 1989, p. 65).

Further, I suggest that professionals are often trained both to aspire to invisibility and to forms of objectivity in respect of others in ways which encourage us to separate ourselves from the experience of the activities in which we engage. I argue that there are consequences, not only for the scientific validity of such research/practices, however, but also for the individuals who are tempted to try and separate themselves from the vitality of their own experience of these practices. Consider the following, from one of the accepted founders of Western science, 'We exist through activity (because we exist by living and acting); and the maker of the work exists, in a sense, through his [*sic*] activity' (Aristotle, 1976, p. 210).

An argument could thus be constructed to suggest that there may be 'psychological' consequences for the individual who would separate themselves from their activity, here engaging in language use. As professionals we may even be tempted to a further position in which, not only can we be separated from our own experiences but we can also be instrumental in separating our clients from the vitality of *their* experiences. Now I would suggest that this is another matter entirely and one which gives rise to serious ethical and moral concerns.

The justifications for separating ourselves, both from and also within our practices is often based on those claims to truth which are themselves based on particular forms of (Western) scientific knowledge. These claims to truth are based on the objective, and by implication, real evidence provided by such methods. However, philosophy can perhaps create another angle from which to view such claims to truth:

> Although there is a connection between objectivity and reality ... not all reality is best understood the more objectively it is viewed. Appearance and perspective are essential parts of what there is, and in some respects they can best be understood from a less detached standpoint. Realism underlines the claims of objectivity and detachment but it supports them only up to a point.
>
> (Nagel, 1986, p. 4)

In this chapter means of analysis are sought which can question those claims to truth and reality which are made in and through language. The search for method here is to be organized around, firstly, historical and economic aspects of experience and narrative, secondly, around the nature and function of speaking and thirdly, following the initial focus upon language, around the idea that 'language, per se, [loses] its centrality as the object to be acquired' (Urwin, in Henriques et al., 1984, p. 287).

I argue further that questions relating to the ownership of knowledge and power are crucial for all who live their lives at this point in world history, including professionals. Retaining ownership of our own individual (hi)stories and experience is a contemporary human (and therefore social) problem which has implications for all our experiences and relationships. It is my contention that professional, and more specifically here, psychological practices can operate to separate people from their experiences by purloining accounts of their lives and by laying claim to greater knowledge and truth – 'Certain speakers, those with training in certain special techniques – supposedly to do with the powers of the mind to make contact with reality – are privileged to speak with authority beyond the range of their personal experience' (Parker and Shotter, 1990, p. 7).

Of Stories

> The act of storytelling is coming to an end ... it is as if something that seemed inalienable to us, the securest among our possessions, were taken from us: the ability to exchange experiences.
>
> (Benjamin, 1992, p. 83)

It can be said that people attempt to make sense of their lives by narrativizing their experiences; people tell stories, both to others and to themselves, not merely through their words but also through their actions. Indeed, 'both conversations in particular and human actions in general [are] enacted narratives' (MacIntyre, 1981, p. 211). Without indulging in any nostalgic yearning, a principal argument here is that in times past, people were more able to retain ownership of their own history by sharing their experiences orally in the telling of stories. It may be helpful to consider at this point Genette's (1980) definitions of three types of narrative:

- the most central in common usage – has narrative refer to the narrative statement, the oral or written discourse that undertakes to tell of an event or series of events;
- less widespread but current today among analysts and theoreticians of narrative content has narrative refer to the succession of events real or fictitious, that are the subjects of this discourse;
- a third meaning, apparently the oldest, has narrative refer once more to an event; not, however, the event that is recounted, but the event that consists of someone recounting something, the act of narrating in itself.

(Genette, 1980, p. 33)

It is this final definition which may prove most helpful here, for it links the methods employed in the book with a more ancient tradition. Genette's third definition of narrative regards the actual activity and manner of recounting events as important and as such it encourages the analyses of those activities in themselves. Professional accounts cannot seek exemption at this point, and in demanding that such accounts remain accessible for analysis there may well be implications for our work with children, in particular here from a psychologist's perspective. For example, it might enable this psychologist/writer to resist becoming totally separated from the activity of authorship, not only in this book but, perhaps more crucially, in the many psychological reports I write, in which I write stories, supposedly of other people.

This approach of examining the activity of narrating itself does not seek either to deny or to support the factual or realist integrity of the events recounted. Rather, it is an approach which demands that the individual author (here the psychologist) should experience primarily in the writing, not the reality of others, but rather the vitality of their own activity which is to write of others.

Paradoxically (and not contradictorily), it may be that, once in contact with our own experience of writing, an author may well be better positioned to make contact with a more reliable, and perhaps even more realist, scientific method. Despite some probable resistance to such methods (a legacy of many practices established in training, both at under- and post-graduate levels), the attempt to reconnect ourselves with our activities is no mere introspection. Indeed, it may be crucial, both to our own well-being and also to the project of an objective science, for it can be argued that, 'Self-understanding is at the heart of objectivity' (Nagel, 1979, p. 78).

It is not only psychologists who can find themselves separated from their own experience, however, for I would argue again that many people become separated from their own stories. On the broader canvas of world history, there are many historians and writers who believe that such fragmentations of experience now permeate all aspects of our (social) lives and activities. I suggest here that this historical evidence is sufficiently compelling to necessitate re-evaluations of current realms of otherwise 'a priori' expertise: '[During the nineteenth century] history and science, so triumphantly combined in the theory of evolution, now found themselves being separated' (Hobsbawm, 1987, p. 269).

That such fragmentations were not always the case is a facet of John Berger's depiction of lives in his trilogy *Pig Earth*. Through his own experiences of living for many years in post-war Alpine village communities, Berger was able to recount stories of lives lived within the last (and fast-disappearing) remnants of an older social order. Berger believed (by implicit comparison with his experience of social life in industrial Europe) that the (real) characters within the villages did not seem to have experienced the kind of disconnection, either from their environment or else from their experiences within that environment, which seems to have afflicted those of us who have only experienced living in a (post-)industrialist society.

In his accounts, Berger also begins to articulate for us the clear distinction between the lives as described in his written accounts and the lives which would be portrayed by the villagers themselves who would use instead the much older tradition of story-telling by word of mouth, 'Until very recently the only material available to a village and its peasants for defining themselves was their own spoken words' (Berger, 1992, p. 9). The historian Hobsbawm supports Berger's position by clarifying for us the significance of the great, historical changes which have occurred both in the social order and in our human relations generally during the last centuries, 'The nineteenth century was the era when oral communication broke down, as the distance between authorities and subjects increased' (1987, p. 149).

Berger seems to articulate the differences in human experience which can exist between orally- and literacy-based communities but Hobsbawm too is sensitive to the historical movements and ramifications. Hobsbawm's additional perspective on the change in human relations not only identifies the historical nature of the separation between the individual and their new society based on mass literacy, but alerts us to the incipient dangers for all our verbal communication, 'From the moment that society rested on mass literacy, a spoken language had to be in some sense official – a medium of bureaucracy and instruction' (1975, p. 156).

At this point I will bring together several aspects of the account: the changing traditions of narrative from oral to written forms; the separation of people from their own accounts of truth and experience; the activity of psychologists and other professionals who work with, and write of other people. Here then, is a short story of people met in the course of my work as a psychologist, Mary and Laura.

A Story of Mary and Laura

Several years ago, I was asked to see an 11-year-old girl in her first year at a high school whose behaviour teachers were finding difficult to manage. I was told by her teachers that Mary was unruly and that her behaviour was bizarre and unacceptable in many different situations. The teachers referred also to Mary's unbelievable tales which she told to the other children and which included one story in which a baby had died at home.

The teachers felt that such story-telling activities were symptomatic of the more general problems Mary seemed to be having, and they were concerned that such stories were affecting her peer relationships, for evidently Mary was constantly making and breaking friendships. However, the teachers knew that Mary did actually have a baby sister, and given both her story and also her record of aggressive behaviour towards other children, they were expressing to me their concerns for the safety of the infant.

Now it also seemed to me that the teachers held views about aspects of Mary's past which in turn affected their attitudes to (and tolerance of) her actual presence in the school. Mary had only recently transferred from the special school which she had attended since she was 6 years old. That special school was designated as a school for children with 'emotional and behavioural difficulties' (an 'EBD' school) and Mary had spent much of her time there as the only girl in the school. Prior to meeting Mary for the first time this was the extent of information that the school could give me. I also had on file, however, a previous psychologist's report which related Mary in terms of a history of social (mis)behaviours, together with several other reports regarding various medical investigations, including her history of epilepsy.

As reader, in the space of those few short paragraphs, you will already have begun to mobilize your own constructs regarding Mary. Also, in view of the three previous chapters of this work you may have begun to create links between this account and the other arguments already set before you, the processes of separating and excluding for example. It is not, however, my intention to deal with the many issues which could arise at this point (although I will return to Mary later in the chapter and also later in the book). Instead, I want to continue with my version of some events as they appeared to me.

My first meeting with Mary lasted about one hour. She chattered away almost non-stop, at times almost breathlessly, in a way which left me puzzled before telling me of some of her anxieties which were connected to bullying in the school (at one point, in a reading exercise she was doing for me, she also read the word 'buried' as 'bullied'. It seems difficult now to avoid a Freudian reading of this; see 'Parapraxes' in Freud, 1973, pp. 50–108).

The meeting seemed to be just part of my working day, and was otherwise largely uneventful. Mary seemed as many other 11-year-old children and on this first occasion neither her social nor her cognitive 'profiles' seemed to reveal anything which I could be expected to regard as hugely significant. I then told Mary that her mother, Laura, was due to come into school to see me in a few minutes, and it was Mary's excitement at the thought of this prospect which demanded my interest. Mary was keen to be there for my meeting with her mother but I asked her if I could see her mother alone first of all and said to Mary that she could join us later on (NB the power of the professional at this point).

Laura, Mary's mother, then spoke to me at some length of Mary's turbulent history. Her story seemed to focus on the frequent medical investigations (for epilepsy), the previous involvement of other psychologists (for bed-wetting and also for unusual behaviour with food – hiding it and storing it in her room) and Mary's often uncontrollable behaviour (for which she had on occasion been taken into the care of social services). I could have stopped Laura from telling all of her story but it seemed important to her. Gradually in the conversation, Laura's dissatisfaction with the various professionals who had been involved with Mary over the years began to surface, 'nobody will tell me what's wrong with her' she said, 'nobody can do anything with her', and more. Again, I could have stopped her, but I used my professional power to encourage her to say just what she wanted. Eventually, Laura decided to make one more effort to tell a professional what she thought was really wrong with Mary:

> *'Nobody ever believes me but I think it was the accident when Mary was ten days old. … I was pushing the pram across the road at a zebra crossing, Mary was in the pram and Michael was on top of it … this car came along and crashed into us. … Mary went flying through the air … when she landed on the ground she didn't move. … I screamed … everyone came rushing up. … I just thought she was dead. … We went into hospital but within a few hours they said that she was alright and discharged her. … After that my milk dried up and I got really bad depression. … I knew she had been alright before that. … I knew from my other children. … Mary was just the same as them. … After the accident it all changed though. … She started with epilepsy at about eighteen months. … She was so bad that my first husband left me. … By the time she was nine her behaviour was so bad that she had split up another relationship. … Now I'm worried that she's going to do the same all over again.'*

Now whether or not we are persuaded of the relevance or validity of Laura's own analysis, I argue that Laura's story has validity 'in itself'. For during her story, not only did I perceive Laura's account to be authentic (why should I suppose otherwise?) but I was also aware of the huge significance to Laura of the events within her story. The story seemed to be hers, told freely. To me, Laura had spoken of human life and death and any reduction or translation of that story into a purely psychologized narrative would seem to be insulting, to Laura and, not least, to Mary. I therefore chose to treat her narrative as valid and tried to give it the respect that it seemed to deserve.

During the next few years I saw Mary on over ten different occasions (the normal service policy is two or three visits per case). On each occasion the pattern was the same, with Mary wanting to draw or write, but all the time talking away non-stop without seeming to demand any responses from me. Mary's presence in school and at home remained tenuous and at times Laura continued to press a variety of professionals for answers. She searched for diagnoses of various kinds of neurological and psychological disturbance, including brain damage, autism and attention deficit/hyperactivity disorder. On the last occasion I met her, however, I reminded her of that story she had told me on the occasion of our first meeting, the story of Mary's accident. She once again seemed to remember the significance of those past events, 'I know she was normal before that … but how can I prove it?'

There are persons who are endeavouring to situate their own lives in preferred stories and to embrace their own knowledge, but who are finding it difficult to do so because of the dominant and disqualifying stories or knowledges that others can have about them and their relationships.

(White, 1989, p. 20)

I argue that Laura had become separated from her own history – by the weight of numerous professionalized and institutionalized re-readings. These re-readings, delivered as they would be by professionals, might well have claimed the power of 'a priori' truths with which some professionals are invested. In their circulation, such accounts offer to the client the tantalizing prospect of a greater truth, a truth greater than the individual or their story, one which can be captured by a professional, authoritative diagnosis.

On occasions when that greater truth is not subsequently offered to the client, however, it may be difficult for the individual to relocate their own truth. So, I would argue, it might have been for Laura. Far from supporting any knowledge of her own that Laura may have had originally, I argue that professional accounts may well have been crucial agents in separating Laura from her own experience and memory which, I would argue, were employed in her story to me. It would seem that Laura's verbal account, so passionately given, has been overwhelmed over the years by the stronger claims to history and truth provided by professionals who were practising *science*.

I suggest that my narrative here provides just one example of the ways in which individual people can become separated from the truth of their own experience through the purloining of those experiences by the representations contained within professionalized accounts. I now want to make a connection, however, the difficulties of which can only be gauged by the size of the gulf which seems to exist between individual people and the sweep of world history. Indeed, the distance between an individual life and world history can appear so great that it can seem ridiculous to attempt to make a connection between the two. Similarly, it can also appear ridiculous to describe those individual lives and experiences such as Mary's and Laura's as either historical or epic in human terms. It is as if the science upon which the various professional accounts would claim to be based cannot tolerate the authoritative oppositions to their own representations of truth which would result from the elevation of experience provided by such a connection.

I suggest that it is not ridiculous to juxtapose Laura's experience and narrative either with Aristotle's concept of a wisdom which can accommodate both intuition *and* science, or with the broad sweep of world history. Benjamin (1992), however, informs us of our fading ability still to access such links, 'the act of storytelling is reaching its end because the epic side of truth, wisdom, is dying out' (Benjamin, 1992, p. 86). Laura had her own knowledge of herself and of her daughter and in telling her story I argue that she shared her wisdom with me. This wisdom seemed to know instinctively that, 'with words everything can happen again ... yet they never change what has happened' (Berger, 1990, p. 190).

To sum up thus far in the chapter: it is important in practices with clients that we resist actions which will hasten the separation of the person, either from their own life histories or from their places in world history. In searching for such processes it may be possible to preserve a language which can enable professionals, not only to encourage others to retain ownership of their experiences, but also to help us to retain ownership of our own. For seeking to retain ownership of our own history has become a radical act within a world history which can otherwise reduce us to states of individual and collective amnesia. 'The truth value of memory lies in the specific function of memory to preserve promises and potentialities which are betrayed and even outlawed by the mature, civilized individual, but which had once been fulfilled in the dim past and which are never entirely forgotten' (Marcuse, 1966, p. 18).

LANGUAGE AND BEYOND

> The history of the subject ... At every point it faces us with the question of how far beyond the relative safety of our present language we can afford to go.
>
> (Nagel, 1986, p. 11)

It has been argued so far that spoken language, through our story-telling, can help us both to retain ownership of our own life experiences and also to resist the alien-ating effects of fractures in our experiential lives which might include, for example, our experiences of working with children. Depending on the stories with which we engage, therefore, it is suggested that spoken words themselves may harbour the very seeds of separation and fragmentation.

I suggest that in reconstructing our own histories or else in encouraging others to reconstruct their own histories, we are working with the stories of material life and we thus need to employ and share the material elements of spoken language. It is appropriate at this point, therefore, to consider briefly some theoretical aspects of language although within the scope of the book it will only be possible to engage in brief speculations. These will, nevertheless, once again seek to juxtapose theoretical aspects of spoken language with examples taken from my practice as an educational psychologist.

Speech acts are, I would argue again, material acts, 'Language may surprise one with its materiality' (Frosh, 1989, p. 120). Its physical nature is also described as follows:

> Speech is in fact a gift of language, and language is not immaterial. It is a subtle body, but body it is. Words are trapped in all the corporeal images that captivate the subject; they make the hysteric 'pregnant', be identified with the object of penis-neid, represent the flood of urine of urethral ambition, or the retained faeces of avaricious jouissance.
>
> (Lacan, 1977, p. 87)

On the one hand, therefore, it is being suggested here that language is a material 'body' which can assist us to retain ownership of our own experiences, whilst on the other hand, it is also being suggested here that language can be a gateway to consideration of what is not language. Georgaca (1995) helps us most succinctly by begging the question posed implicitly by all language when she asks, 'Are there things beyond language?'

Earlier in the chapter I suggested that I was inclined to believe both Laura's description of events and her own assessment of their significance. To what extent, however, could I experience either those events recounted, or else share her feelings about their importance? In other words, to what extent could the words used by Laura be used again by me to re-experience totally and exactly, as for Laura, those earlier events and feelings experienced subjectively? Such an accurate empathy would seem unlikely, and this rejection of a precise verbal communication therefore brings into question the exactitude of words and again leads us towards questions concerning the beyond of language. I suggest that, both for the transmitter and for the receiver of words, not only will the experience of the materiality of the language be different for the participants, but also that any representations and meanings which lie inside or beyond the language will have different components too. This would accord with Lacan's (psychoanalytic) observance of the 'success of miscommunication' (in Hollway, 1989, p. 19).

Indeed, psychoanalysis has been a discrete branch of psychology which has often acted as a depository for the beyond of language. More recently, however, some psychoanalysts have become alert to the ways in which, through language, they represent this 'beyond', for example, in the works of Lacan (1977) (see also the works of the clinical psychologist Stephen Frosh, 1987 and 1989). Other psychoanalysts have reflected upon their own practices and have also raised similar questions concerning either the reliability or else the precision of words, as I have just done with Laura's account; for example, 'the wish that words could be a "tabula rasa" keeping only the meaning individuals ask of them is a mad wish' (Sinason, 1988, p. 226).

During the twentieth century language became a more central concern for scholarly exploration (e.g. Wittgenstein, Chomsky) but whilst speech and language have been important to various branches of psychology, the meaning of words has offered researchers in psychology a less secure field of operation. Indeed, hermeneutics seems to be a site of human investigation which psychology has not yet acquired from philosophers and literary scholars. Vygotsky went as far to say that, 'word meaning has been lost in the ocean of all other aspects of consciousness ... contemporary psychology has ... no specific ideas regarding word meaning' (Vygotsky, 1986, p. 5).

Recent approaches to discourse analysis, however, have brought questions of meaning, again initially through language, once more within reach of a broader psychology. These approaches have revived possibilities for psychology to keep in touch with a range of intellectual activities, including politics, psychoanalysis, literature and philosophy, for example. In so doing I would argue that such forms of discourse analysis have resisted the historical tide which, increasingly, has been demanding fragmented specializations.

Speculations on Speaking and Meaning

Prior to consideration of conversations with Mary and her mother Laura, the three following short citations provide some further analytical possibilities which could be applied in order to enhance professional practice.

* Firstly, Lev Vygotsky, the inter-war Russian developmental psychologist (whose work only became widely known in Western countries during the 1960s) insisted that the need for social contact is the trigger and continuing function of language – 'The primary function of speech, in both children and adults, is communicative, social contact' (Vygotsky, 1986, p. 34).
* Secondly, the contemporary American psychologists and therapists Fred Newman and Lois Holzman place an emphasis here upon the link between language and a human quest which is to make sense of our lives in a search for meaning – 'Meaning-making [is the] historical pre-condition for language making' (Newman and Holzman, 1993, p. 113).
* Lastly, Wilfred Bion, the post-war child psychiatrist and psychoanalyst suggests that language is also linked to various somatic (and by implication material) processes – '[the original function of verbal thought] – providing restraint for motor discharge' (Bion, 1962, p. 57).

Whilst all the above statements emanate from different psychological and historical points of reference I argue here, therefore, not for a theory of language based upon any single one of the above statements but for a theory of language which can tolerate aspects of them all. At first, the statements may appear to some extent incompatible and my argument vainly eclectic. For example, it seems that implicit within Vygotsky's speech acts is the existence of a pre-condition within individuals which drives us to make contact with other people. Newman and Holzman's theory of language focuses upon our attempts to make sense of experience whilst Bion's account of speaking here rests upon a verbal thinking which links our physical and psychological worlds.

In a world which, increasingly, seems to offer people a bewildering array of choices, a theory of language which resists the allure of simplistic and reductionist analytic accounts is likely to meet with some resistance. This may especially be the case when attempts are made to link a more complex theory with day-to-day practices in the field with clients. Nevertheless, I suggest that there is room in a theory of language for all of the apparently differing statements made by Vygotsky, Newman and Holzman and also Bion. I also suggest that child professionals could seek to resist simplistic analyses when reductionism merely masks a ruthless pragmatism. Which brings me back to Laura and Mary.

For the terms of my employment do not require me to consider complex or difficult models and indeed in practice no such time is allowed. Initially, I had been asked by the school, in essence, to 'get rid of' Mary's bizarre behaviour. What if that behaviour *is* the child? The question with which I am supposed to confront myself in professional practice would usually be, 'how can I get rid of Mary's bizarre behaviour?' Well, should this be the focus of my work, the proper unit of study (after Vygotsky) or should it be to find out more of what is happening and what is being represented? It is through language that this may become possible but this does not offer the professional the quick-fix preferred by many modern practices. Within this book, however, I have created a little more time with which to consider Mary, Laura and, not least, my own actions.

In Laura's original account to me of the accident, I had experiences which, in part, were a response to her words – I was hearing, feeling, conceptualizing. I assume now that, prior to those experiences of mine, there was at least a part of Laura that chose to employ those certain words as a consequence of my presence. Laura's words were born between us, therefore, within a social context which allowed them to exist, at least in part, as a means of communication between us.

The words Laura spoke were also material acts, for I heard them and they consumed time. The words did not appear as words chosen at random, and they were put together in a way that offered her the prospect of a contact with another person. They were words which, however, through their qualitative resonances, also offered the prospect of meaning, both for Laura and for myself. The words Laura used, therefore, were acts which were material and as such they could be communicative; they could also, I would argue, provide evidence of 'psychological' activity as well as meanings: 'Talking must be considered as potentially two different activities, one as a mode of communication and the other as the employment of the musculature to disencumber the personality of thoughts' (Bion, 1962, p. 83).

Taking the first of Bion's 'two activities', Bion appears to restrict the communicative possibilities to a singular 'mode'. However, there may be several communicative possibilities offered by speaking. For example, the object of communication may be social contact-in-itself, or its focus may be rather the expression of meaning in representational form. Neither of these possibilities would conflict with Vygotsky's model. Bion's second suggested 'activity' within language, however, suggests that individuals use language as a physical means of coping with psychological anxieties, as evacuations from the 'psyche', and this would not at first sight appear to be a reconcilable hypothesis. Before I consider this 'economic' position further, however, I would like to dwell a little longer on the communicative aspects of speaking.

Vygotsky's overall view was of a general direction of development from social to private speech. Whilst we are used to employing a model of the social which implies an 'other', is that 'other' necessarily another person, or could the 'other' with whom we need to make (social) contact be within us? 'For the function of language is not to inform but to evoke. What I seek in language is the response of the other' (Lacan, 1977, p. 86).

In Laura's description of the accident, I might infer that her account was intended to be, at least in part, broadly communicative. There were certain moments, however, when in her telling of the story, it seemed as though Laura was neither looking to communicate with me nor did she appear to require a response from me. It did seem, however, that she was looking to evoke some kind of response, from some 'other'. I suggest that this 'other' was within Laura herself for by the time that she said to me, '*I just thought she was dead*', although her language still seemed to retain both social and communicative elements, it did not seem that she was looking for a reply from me. It is possible that she wanted to share this knowledge with me, i.e. she did not necessarily want to tell me but she may have wanted me to know.

I suggest further, however, that Laura might well have been talking to herself, and that both the social and the communicative elements operated not outside of her but within her. This view would then, perhaps, concur with a further aspect of Vygotsky's account of spoken language, for his 'egocentric speech' would provide just such a model for an 'inner speech'.

I argue, therefore that, in recounting the events of Mary's accident to me, Laura was not merely communicating with me, she was communicating with herself. In the process she was evoking the 'other' within herself whilst at the same time leading me to my own acts of meaning-making, perhaps with my 'other'. Through her account, in those material, communicative and psychological activities, perhaps Laura had also thus begun to communicate with, and therefore re-create meaning for herself, as well as in the process perhaps just wanting someone else to know.

This begins to suggest that there was an authenticity in our exchange and although I was not offering her an easy pathology for Mary's behaviour, I believe that I could have been helping Laura to re-create an important, vital and human experience for herself. I would argue that for a few moments at least Laura was able to own again something of her history which was achieved in part and paradoxically, through the knowing that I knew also.

Such possibilities then lead us back to Newman and Holzman's affirmation of the importance of meaning-making within language. But if communication and meaning-making are both functions of language, we need a view as to how they work.

Symbol

> Symbol formation governs the capacity to communicate, since all communication is made by means of symbols.
>
> (Segal, 1986, p. 169)

Contemporary psychoanalysis has again provided a site for informed speculative accounts, this time regarding the necessity of symbolic life as a pre-condition for language, communication and meaning-making. Freud's first major recognizably psychoanalytic text was, to a large extent, based on the accounts of symbolism within his theory of dreams (in particular, for example, Freud, 1976, pp. 461–540). Melanie Klein also placed symbol formation as an integral part of her theories, in particular of 'object-relations' (see Klein [1932], 1989, p. 147). More recently other psychoanalysts have made more specific links between our symbolic lives and language, Segal (1986) and Lacan (1977), for example, whilst 'Language is taken by both Lacan and Kristeva as the exemplary form of the symbolic signifying system that structures the human universe' (Georgaca, 1995, p. 2).

The principal inferences now are that, firstly, our symbolic lives predate our use of language and that, secondly, language itself is a symbolic form. As such, psychoanalysis has suggested a model of language which not only offers us the means of symbolizing and representing our experiences of the external world and of communicating with it, but it also offers through symbolism the means of understanding more of our internal communication: 'Symbols are needed not only in communication with the external world but also in internal communication' (Segal, 1986, p. 169).

It is suggested then, not only that there exist within us inner communications and meanings, but also that something of these communications can be known through our symbol-formation and language. Segal goes on to link the processes of internal communication with symbolism which together become the very basis of verbal thinking.

> The capacity to communicate with oneself by using symbols is, I think, the basis of verbal thinking – which is the capacity to communicate with oneself by means of words. Not all internal communication is verbal thinking, but all verbal thinking is an internal communication by means of symbols – words.
>
> (Segal, 1986, p. 169)

So the claim is not made that all inner communication is verbal but it is claimed that all words are themselves evidence of an internal communication, via symbolic means. Within psychoanalysis the possibilities of thinking, speaking and meaning which are suggested by such concepts open considerable analytical and temporal complexities. For simplicity's sake, these complexities can be reduced here to:

- condensation – the compression of several meanings within one symbol and;
- displacement – the mobility of a single meaning across a variety of different symbols.

Lacan (1977, following the work of Jakobson, 1962 and Saussure, 1974) described means of linguistic analysis based on a structure of 'signifiers' and 'signified'. Stephen Frosh (1987), drawing on Lacan, likened the linguistic concepts of metaphor and metonymy through which the signifiers and signified of language could operate, to the concepts of condensation and displacement within psychoanalysis; metaphor was seen as a linguistic equivalent to condensation whilst metonymy was the linguistic equivalent to psychoanalytic displacement. Essentially this model suggests that a single symbol or word ('signifier') can contain several different representations ('signified') and also that individual representations ('signifieds') can re-locate themselves along a linear temporal plane within different symbols or words ('signifiers'). The various works cited above – Jakobson, Lacan, and Frosh, and also Hollway, 1989 – suggest that we might be able to access aspects of Laura's account as in Figure 4.1.

So when Laura said to me that '*I just thought she was dead*', at least three more possibilities now come to mind. Firstly, although I have already suggested that the words would be a form of internal communication, to what extent could I interpret them as speaking for themselves? For, secondly, did any of the individual symbols/words contain a compression of various representations of which I might not be aware? Or,

Figure 4.1

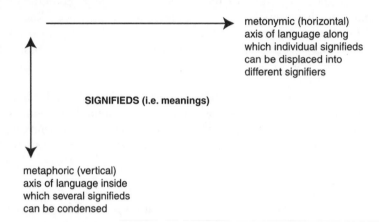

SIGNIFIERS (i.e. words)

`Everyone came rushing up. . . I just thought she was dead`

metonymic (horizontal)
axis of language along
which individual signifieds
can be displaced into
different signifiers

SIGNIFIEDS (i.e. meanings)

metaphoric (vertical)
axis of language inside
which several signifieds
can be condensed

thirdly, could there have been just one pre-occupying representation which lived inside all the audible symbols/words and which moved along the linear, metonymic axis? For example, we are led to questions such as, *who* was dead and in what ways, physically or emotionally? There may be another element which can illuminate the above possibilities.

Vygotsky considered 'egocentric speech' to post-date communicative speaking with others and this idea led to my previous suggestion that Laura's words, if indeed they could be seen as an internal communication, would be evidence of her own developmental maturity. Contemporary psychoanalysis, however, has been placing the development of our internal symbolic lives prior to the development of a language shared with others, 'Symbol formation starts very early, probably as early as object-relations' (Segal, 1986, p. 163).

During the twentieth century psychoanalysts gradually modified their assumptions as to when various important processes could first be seen during infancy. Overall, the tendency was to attribute a number of processes to earlier stages of development, for example the formation of the ego (see Klein, 1989). Indeed, some of the most recent psychoanalytic studies have begun to go back even further and focus on the significance of intra-uterine developments (for example, Piontelli, 1992).

I now argue several points which allow for the existence of both the 'pre-linguistic' of infancy and also the 'extra-linguistic' of child and adulthood.

- Firstly, I argue that symbolic life is a pre-condition of linguistic development which begins to occur at a very early stage, alongside our internal ego development and together with our relationship to objects in our environment: 'Melanie Klein came to the conclusion that if symbolisation did not occur, the whole development of the ego is arrested … symbolism is … a relation between the ego, the object and the symbol' (Segal, 1986, p. 163).

- Secondly, I argue that the development of symbolic life is itself evidence that a separation has occurred between our experience and our representations of those experiences, thus providing us with an omni-present, internal, but social, 'other': 'The gap between the ego and the drive motility establishes a place of lack that the Other, the realm of language will fill up with the Oedipus complex' (Georgaca, 1995, p. 20).

- Thirdly, I argue that this suggested split between the real of our experiences and our symbolic representations of those experiences is forged through dual inter-actions, one which is an internal relationship and one which is our relationship with the external world: 'Symbol formation and the anxiety it is built upon are thus crucial components of early development … and also the source of the child's relationship to reality' (Frosh, 1989, p. 137).

Lalangue

Symbol formation, I suggest therefore, is a process which, from a very early age, constantly allows us to represent our experiences of both our internal and external worlds.

I would suggest, therefore, that symbol formation is also evidence of a primary separation, which is the subject of this book; that it occurs not only between ourselves and our environment, but occurs also as a separation within ourselves, between our unconscious knowledge of our experiences and our representations of those experiences of which we can become aware in our consciousness. I also suggest that it is both the qualitative and economic aspects of these processes of separating and splitting in which identities are formed, 'Lacan makes splitting the fundamental developmental process. … Lacan focuses on alienation, on how the subject becomes formed in "otherness", how identity is always produced by the insertion of subject into something outside' (Frosh, 1987, p. 129).

Psychoanalysis, after Freud, has considered processes of splitting and separating in a variety of different forms and with different results. For example, Bowlby's post-Second World War adaptation of Kleinian 'object-relations' was employed strategically by institutional forces – in this case the government (see Riley, 1983). Indeed, a focus for post-war British psychology in general was the initial develop-ment of a child through its relationship with its mother. Psychoanalysis in particular provided a site for society to examine these processes and such studies came to consider the ways in which children separate from their mothers. 'According to Klein, the motivating power for the accomplishment of symbolism is anxiety … defensively projected on to an external object' (Frosh, 1989, p. 136).

I now argue that Mary's accident when she was but a few days old may well have had a serious effect upon her mother and, through Mary's experience of her mother, may then have had a serious effect upon her, notwithstanding any physical damage which may have occurred as a result of head injuries. Lacanian analysts would take the position that it is 'the mirror-phase that opens up the possibility of the symbolic' (Georgaca, 1995, p. 4) and that what exists for a child in the mirror-phase, pre-linguistically (and pre-symbolically) is 'lalangue'. 'Lalangue is best defined as the maternal language. Language as a signifying system is built on lalangue' (ibid., p. 27).

I suggest that one way of seeing Mary and her mother can be provided by such psychoanalytic texts. For what if, at just a few days old, Mary's lalangue, her experience of a maternal language, suffered a catastrophe, a near-destruction? The evidence can be amassed as follows.

Firstly, there was the violence of the physical sensations which she would have experienced as a baby thrown through the air together with the crash of the impact. Secondly, that which she might not even have known as 'not her' – her mother, Laura – was suddenly gone. Thirdly, that this loss of what had been until that moment 'her' could have been akin to experiencing a particularly sudden and savage death. Fourthly, this experience could have demanded either a mirror-phase or a symbolic life for which she might have been ill-prepared in the usual developmental terms. Finally, Mary's experience of loss of her mother (herself) in such a way could have been felt as permanent for, although Laura was only separated from Mary for a few hours, the fact that her milk then dried up could have symbolized a variety of other serious psychological, as well as physical responses for them both.

It may even be the case that Mary has also since the accident harboured the 'real' of her experiences of that time in a way that has offered little hope of acquiring a symbolic language which can make that 'real' tolerable for her. Although in any case, 'the real is that part of the external world which the symbolic cannot reach' (Georgaca, 1995, p. 8), it may be that Mary's experience affected her whole acquisition of a symbolic life which could have allowed her to deal with her pain more easily. 'The symbol is used not to deny but to overcome loss' (Frosh, 1987, p. 138, after Segal).

I wrote earlier that on the first occasion I met Mary she just chattered away non-stop, and this continued to be the pattern of our meetings. It was almost as if the words Mary used were totally dissociated from their usual representations; but it was also the case that Mary seemed not to talk to me but to an 'other' who was present for her. These may be crucial factors in any story of Mary and I am reminded here of Bion's observations of language and experience:

> A word contains a meaning; conversely, a meaning can contain a word – which may or may not be discovered. The relationship is established by the nature of the link. A constant conjunction of elements in a psychoanalysis can be 'bound' by the attribution to it of a word, a theory, or other formulation. The word by which it is bound can have such a powerful pre-existing penumbra of associations that it squeezes the life out of the constant conjunction it is supposed to mark. Conversely, the constant conjunction can destroy the word, theory or other formulation that the formulation is intended to 'contain'. For example, a man [sic] is attempting to express such powerful feelings that his capacity for verbal expression disintegrates into a stammer or a meaningless, incoherent babble of words.
>
> (Bion, 1970, p. 106)

This perhaps is what I experienced when with Mary for it seemed that her words, although empty of their usual meanings, were that 'incoherent babble' through which she was trying to communicate the enormity of her feelings. She may well have been trying to 'disencumber' her anxieties through her musculature. Perhaps then, Laura had been right all along and her story was authentic. Perhaps she always knew what we professionals could not see. For perhaps in different ways, Mary did die in the accident; for that part of Laura which was Mary might have died in Laura, whilst that part of Mary which was Laura might have died in her also. Perhaps Mary is constantly reliving her own death, therefore, which was, in part, the death of her mother and as such no matter what the situation, Mary is constantly being overpowered by her experience of her own unbearable 'real'. 'The real is that part of the external world which the symbolic cannot reach ... the real is the limit of our experience ... that radical otherness that haunts our existence' (Georgaca, 1995, pp. 8–16).

I believe that it was, in part, my 'intuition', my sensing of that unbearability in Mary's experience which encouraged me to maintain contact with Laura and Mary over several years. In this contact I sought to retain some ownership of the vitality which was my experience of contact with them; for although the focus could easily rest upon Mary's unbearable real, it allowed me to keep hold of my sensing of that unbearability – a sensing which was my own.

Endpiece

In this chapter, therefore, I have sought a means of retaining ownership of the stories which I have told (NB: I continue these stories later). I have sought, not to usurp the accounts of Laura and Mary, but rather to base my story upon the evidence of their accounts whilst at the same time exploring theoretical means of supporting my experience of those representations of their own truth. 'When we conceive of the minds of others, we cannot abandon the essential factor of a point of view; instead we must generalize it and think of ourselves as one point of view among others' (Nagel, 1986, p. 20).

The process in which I have engaged could lead, I believe, to a more scientific method than that which would have otherwise been demanded of me in the course of my employment as an educational psychologist. I would claim that this story of Laura and Mary has been my own and that its reflections and speculations are scientific, supported by psychoanalytic and linguistic texts. Before considering the ways in which written language might hold possibilities for alternative 'ways of seeing', the following literary quotation might on the one hand affirm particular representations of Mary's experiences but might also on the other hand provide some illumination upon the ways in which our separations can become concretized within the authority of a written language:

> In the school there [at Cluses] I learnt to look at words like something written on a blackboard. When a man [*sic*] swears, the words come out of his body like

shit. As kids we talk like that all the time. ... At Cluses I learnt that words belonged to writing. We used them; yet they were never entirely our own.

(Berger, 1989, p. 123)

Perhaps during my sessions with Mary and Laura, I had provided a space within which they could reconnect with earlier experiences. In resisting a professional attack upon their chosen means of expression, I had perhaps avoided compounding any fragmentations and provided them each with a safe place in which to 'shit'.

Suggestions for Further Reading

Lev Vygotsky (1986) continues to provide a rich source of ideas relating to the origins and functions of language.

Jacques Lacan, a French psychoanalyst, challenges many prevailing assumptions about language (see *Écrits*, 1977).

Michael White continues to explore the use of narratives in his therapeutic work with young people, often in educational settings (see White, 1989, White and Epston, 1990 and also McLean, 1995, *Dulwich Centre Newsletters*).

5   Authority and the Written Word

I am a writer: my writing is both a link and a barrier. I have never thought of writing as a profession. It is a solitary independent activity in which practice can never bestow seniority. Fortunately anyone can take up the activity. Whatever the motives, political or personal, which have led me to undertake to write something, the writing becomes, as soon as I begin, a struggle to give meaning to experience. Every profession has limits to its competence, but also its own territory. Writing as I know it, has no territory of its own. The act of writing is nothing except approaching the experience written about; just as, hopefully, the act of reading the written text is a comparable act of approach.

(Berger, 1992, p. 6)

In the previous chapter the spoken word was subjected to scrutiny, both theoretical and applied. In this chapter, however, it is written words which are subjected to critical analysis. Of the vast numbers of words written about children each year by all those involved in the children industry (for example, teachers, administrators, paediatricians, psychologists, social workers and various therapists), I select just a few professional accounts from my casework. Theoretical considerations are applied which link the words used to particular practices and outcomes for the children concerned and are not intended to provide sites for an individualized blame.

Introduction

Writing constitutes a substantial part of my activity as a psychologist working with children. Reflecting upon the words I use in writing of children, however, certain questions come to mind; for example, not only '*how* should I write?' but more especially the question 'how should I write of another person?'

I argue that these questions provide sites for serious theoretical and ethical issues which require analysis. If, as Berger suggested, written words are 'never entirely our own', are there not also difficult questions concerning the activity of writing itself which child professionals need to address? For if words do not completely belong to the writer, to whom do they belong? In a report on a child, for example, do the words belong to the writer, to the (child) subject, or else do they belong to the presenting (adult) authority which requested them? If, again as Berger suggests, '[written] words belong to writing' where is the writer? Once this question becomes available to analyses of professional/psychologized accounts, however, the question, 'where is the person of whom the words have been written?' follows quickly. These are crucial questions, for if the writer's presence in the words is analytically vague, what grounds are there for believing that the (child) subject exists in the words which supposedly provide a truthful and accurate account. Thus, to what extent can the words written in psychologists' (professional) texts carry something, let alone the truth of another person?

Writing and the Written Word

Berger's argument above (for example, writing is 'a struggle to give meaning to experience') allows reflection upon any temptations to represent as simple truths those stories of individuals which occur in this book. Berger's views on writing also coincide in part with Genette's third definition of narrative (see p. 37), which places an emphasis on the activity and vitality of the act of narrating itself and, through specifying a connection between meaning and experience, Berger provides a reminder that the meanings and experiences which form the narrative in this book are my own creation (although as reader you perform further narrative acts of your own) so the acts of narrating here in the written words are evidence of my own struggle.

In exposing my own subjective experience of writing here, however, in particular regarding questions of accuracy or veracity, I am performing a reflexive activity which is normally unwanted by those who have the power to request my psychological reports. Indeed, LEAs require (and training courses can encourage) an 'objective' language which seeks to deny the presence of an author.

Processes of Formal Assessment under the Education Acts (1981, 1993, 1996) facilitate further disconnections between professionals and their activities of authorship. For example, the reports which I write for a child under this Act are subsumed within an overall professionalized account (the Statement) in which questions of authorship and ownership can be complex. I argue that such questions are problematic, for the institutions and agencies which operate at the legal edge of child definition and control protect the subjective identities of those who actually compile the 'Statements of Special Needs' in a web of institutional and professional power relations.

To 'Statement' a child is (as well as being a verb) a definitive act of production within the enterprise of child regulation and control. A 'Statement' (as a noun) can be evidence of a decisive moment in the enactment of a child's exclusion from areas of social life and it requires little analytical sophistication to comprehend its authoritative potentials. It is unequivocal; it allows no doubt or question, it is a 'Statement' – supposedly of fact. In effect a 'Statement' says, this *is* the particular child in question. At the same time, however, it permits the invisibility of those who would write so authoritatively about the child. In order to cast analytical light on our acts of writing, consider the following concepts relating to the process of writing:

- Writing is speech without an interlocutor, addressed to an absent or imaginary person or to no one in particular (Vygotsky, 1986, p. 182);

- Communication in writing ... is addressed to an absent person who rarely has in mind the same subject as the writer (ibid., p. 240);
- Texts speak in the absence of speakers ... meaning detached from local contexts of interpretation (Smith, 1988, p. 40).

All these comments on the nature of writing and the written word would seem especially pertinent in the case of LEA Statements of children's needs. In this book I am endeavouring, as far as I am able, to remain visible to the (absent and unknown) reader by reflecting upon my 'struggle' to bring 'meaning to experience'. An LEA Statement, however, is invested with such power that it can protect its authors from those questions of ownership to which I am submitting myself here. A 'Statement' is invested with such authority that it need not declare its authors, indeed it might begin to appear that there is some correlation between the degree of authorial invisibility and the power of a text.

Now all Statements possess an LEA officer's signature. There would, therefore, appear to be an author. However, the words in a Statement emanate from a variety of sources, none of which are declared. Further, these sources are protected from having to disclose their authorial position and are allowed to avoid any questions of 'struggle', 'meaning' or 'experience'. Such contests can be made more visible, however, by adopting narrative analyses which can be found in literary texts (for example, Berger and Genette). It is writers, therefore, who can remind child professionals of the nature of our vital activity when we write of children.

It is the apparent absence of these contests, however, which allows certain texts to appear unequivocal, and their authority is enhanced by the apparent separation of the texts from their human origins. The aridity which seems to characterize such texts also allows them to claim a univocality of which now even sole authors would be wary. For example, this book has been written by a me who can have many facets and positions which move across time and space; the words which appear in a Statement, however, whilst selected by an individual LEA 'officer', are often compiled from a variety of individual professional accounts and yet claim singular truths about a child.

A principal source of the words which are found in Statements, however, is the report produced by the LEA psychologist. I argue that the source and selection of the words which can appear in Statements (together with the effectiveness of their disguise) give rise to many issues which have theoretical and practical significance. Consideration of these questions, and the selective 'purloining' of others' words and letters within Statements, also begins to shed light on the limitations demanded of/imposed upon the original professional author – in my case as psychologist.

There are aspects of all written accounts which, notwithstanding all efforts to make visible individual authorship, make available questions of time, place and meaning. Such questions are prompted by the 'turn to language' and, in this chapter, through possibilities offered by discourse analytic approaches. In Genette's three definitions of narrative, he outlines further the temporal complexities of any written account, 'Narrative is a doubly temporal sequence. ... There is the time of the thing told and the time of the narrative (the time of the signified and the time of the signifier) … [there is] an opposition between story time and narrative time' (Genette, 1980, p. 33).

A Statement is an act of authority whose properties are such that it can confirm a pathology in law:

> *The Statement, I suggest, is a defining moment in the process of pathologizing children which is performed within existing social relations. It is a marking point in a process of power relations in which individual children can be separated and excluded with clinical precision.*

In Chapter 3 I examined powers which are invested in categorizations, powers which make more likely long-term restrictions upon the kinds of social and economic activities in which young people such as Mary will be able to engage. As a legal document, the Statement allows the pathology to move along the metonymic axis, across time and place, making Mary, for example, permanently available to executive powers as a person with 'special needs'.

Mary's Statement

A 'Statement' can thus represent many different stories, stories which will have been told by different people at different times. For example, in Mary's 'Statement', the views of several people will have been sought under the legal requirements of the Act – the headteacher, a medical doctor, the parents, a psychologist as a minimum. Many of the words incorporated into Mary's 'Statement', however, are taken almost exclusively from my report.

There is a section in her 'Statement' which attempts to describe Mary and her needs. This section is 271 words long, virtually all of which are taken verbatim from the report which I produced for the assessment. My original description of Mary was about 1,200 words long, however, and it therefore becomes possible to consider which of my words the LEA officer chose to omit, but also the few that the officer chose to replace with (presumably) their own. I now refer to five short, textual extracts taken from my report written about Mary and taken also from her final 'Statement'.

Firstly, the officer's description of Mary begins with words which were not mine, *'Mary is a pupil of low average abilities whose attainments in the basic skills are roughly commensurate with her abilities.'* This is in contrast to my description which began, *'Mary is a young person who has cognitive abilities within the expected range. Her attainments in the basic skills, literacy and numeracy, are roughly commensurate with her abilities.'*

Just as in the case of Gary in Chapter 2, I had sought to use psychometric results as resistance on Mary's behalf, seeking to ward off the pathological gaze of abnormality by asserting the 'normality' of her scores and highlighting her strengths. Once again, this resistance had itself been rejected, deemed as it must have been, an inappropriate professional judgement. The officer in question must have searched through the thick file until they found a different opinion, for *'low average abilities'* is a phrase which can be found in a previous psychological report.

My efforts to place Mary's ability as commonplace, therefore (which is itself made possible by the language of 'scientific' probability), had been rejected in favour of a more pathological form which confines her place hierarchically (a hierarchical placement which is also made possible by the 'scientific' model). I would argue, then, that the form of resistance which I employed here is limited as it fails to challenge either of the fundamental discourses of 'ability' or 'achievement' which are essential resources for the pathologizing tendency.

A second analytic possibility in this extract is the counter-resistance to my own resistance in which I had attributed to Mary a common humanity as a *'young person'*. This too must have been deemed undesirable, for the 'Statement' instead refers to Mary as a *'pupil'*, which whilst not unreasonable in itself, is structurally weaker in this instance.

Thirdly, any attempts in my report to represent either Mary's or Laura's evidence were always omitted from the Statement. For example, in one section of my report of about 100 words, only the following words of mine were omitted in the final Statement, *'Some of Mary's difficulties in adapting to mainstream education have also been connected to her own sense of shame at having previously attended a "Special" school.'* Now any assertion of Mary's sensibilities is likely to be problematic and, whilst my representations of her may possibly contain truths, my words – *'Mary's sense of shame'* – should themselves remain open to critical analysis as *my* narrative for 'Objective reality must be denied to what has been experienced subjectively' (Haug, 1992, p. 20).

I suggest here, however, that my words might have met with disapproval for reasons other than the ones made available by Haug. For whilst Haug is questioning any claims to truth which I make as a psychologist regarding Mary's subjective experience, perhaps the officer may not merely be undermining my representation of Mary's subjective life, for the effect is to challenge Mary's right to possess such a life within her institutionalized 'career' in the LEA. Essentially I was attempting to attribute Mary with an emotional sensitivity. It is this which, I argue, was being rejected by the 'Statement'. It is in this way that the refinements, or indeed just the possession itself of subjective experience, can often be denied by adults in relation to selected young people. Pupils, therefore, especially pathologized pupils, will only be permitted to possess those subjective sensibilities which are allowed by adult authority figures. My representation of Mary's *'sense of shame'* had been a ploy to present her as a person who is capable of an experiential life with the same characteristics as anybody else, including by implication, any adults in authority. My attempt to elevate Mary through sensitive appreciation of her experiences, however, had once again been spotted.

The fourth piece of textual evidence I present here brings into question a censor's own emotional life. For I suggest that s/he might not have enjoyed the precise connection I make between attendance at a special school and its emotional ramifications for the individual child 'client'. Some professionals can spend each day of their working lives allocating many such *'pupils'* to various forms of 'special' education. That their endeavours might lead to 'shameful' experiences for the pathologized children might well be a knowledge which would be resisted by an individual officer. The omission of Mary's 'sense of shame', however, might not have been a consequence of the censor's own emotional confusion but might instead have represented a more aggressive impulse. For as professionals we might be persuaded of the 'hope' that discourses of 'special needs' offer, of specialist and individual help. Whatever intent can be supposed, however, the act of omission is an act of authority.

A fifth analytical contest concerns the following words taken from my description of Mary, words which were removed from a section which otherwise appears intact in the Statement. *'It is important, therefore, that all adults in her life consider Mary's behaviour in terms of her social insecurities and find ways to minimize her anxieties, particularly at times of conflict.'* This is my attempt to place responsibility for any future misdemeanour attributed to Mary within a wider social context. It would seem that I am trying here to explore the possibilities of employing Mary's status as a child to invoke adult protection and responsibility. Once again, however, my attempt to undermine the pathologizing process has been spotted and removed from the Statement. Having previously denied Mary as a 'young person', Mary is now denied as a child, for that might invoke popular feelings and discourses of vulnerability and protection. It would seem that there is an 'insistence' (after Lacan) within the processes of pathologization that Mary face the (punitive) consequences of her behaviour and governmentality can regulate the individual resistances available.

I argue that the Statementing process is one in which the adults who had a structural, social responsibility for Mary, her teachers, doctors and social workers, her psychologist even, will be allowed to separate themselves from her and sever their responsibilities to her. The 'Statement', therefore, whilst a defining moment in a child's life, is supported by processes in which the professionals too become defined by their activities. Once again, however, the peripatetic nature of the pathologizing processes can tempt us to apportion blame solely to individual professionals – a consequence of which would be the concealment of the insistence of governmentality.

Ownership and Power

At different times in the previous section I found myself allocating ownership of the text to the LEA. According to Derrida, however, in his critique of Poe's short story 'The purloined letter' (1975), questions of authority and ownership relating to the written word can be complex. It is in the quest for official truths, I would suggest after Derrida, that a text can find itself with, 'no owner. It is no-one's property. It has no proper meaning, no proper content which bears on its trajectory' (Derrida, 1975, p. 42). The text produced by the LEA, although casually referred to as Mary's 'Statement', does not actually belong to her. It is not her property. Mary's voice, if it is heard at all, is indeed faint. To whom, then, does Mary's Statement belong, if not to her?

As a legal document, under the law, the 'Statement' is the property of the LEA. But to whom do the individual words belong? Do they belong to the LEA officer who selected the words for the 'Statement' among all other evidence, or do the words included in the 'Statement' belong to the original authors? Certainly I am already wanting to distance myself from ownership of any of the words which appear in Mary's 'Statement' for can I not claim, at the very least, that the selection of individual words at the expense of others by a third party, the LEA officer, will distort the meanings for which I 'struggled' in my original narrative?

Should we allow that the LEA officer had their own struggle to give meaning to experience and, if so, what was its nature? Certainly, the officer would seek some immunity should the Statement be subjected to investigation or legal challenge, and it is possible that, at this point, they would seek concealment behind any individual authorial source. The web of structures of meaning which would ensue from any such contest would be so complex, however, as to undermine any truths which could result.

I argue that the words in Mary's Statement clearly do not belong to Mary and also that they have no direct claim upon the truth of Mary's life. The source of the Statement's power is as a 'statutory' report and as such it appropriates ownership of the truth by virtue of its power. The Statement's primary claim to truth, therefore, lies in its status as an official report. It is important, however, that any analysis should not only consider the report but the structured power relations in which the report is produced for, 'If only the dialogue's meaning as a report is retained, its verisimilitude may appear to depend on a guarantee of exactitude' (Lacan, 1972, p. 47).

A Statement's authority is enhanced because it claims exactitude and denies individual authorship within processes of power relations. There are dangers, therefore, in constantly pursuing linguistic arguments without, at the same time, considering what is being overlooked and discourse analytic approaches adopted, for example, by Burman et al. (1996), Parker et al. (1995) and this author (1995, 2000) are concerned not only with language but with the power relations which exist beyond the words. Indeed, there is a danger, 'in the attention only to language at the expense of an attention to the materiality of power. Although power is actively (re)produced in discourse, power is also at work in the structural position of people, when they are not speaking. Power relations endure when the text stops' (Parker, in Burman and Parker, 1993, p. 158).

A discourse analytic approach, therefore, may allow us to see that it is not the words in themselves which necessarily hold the truths about Mary, nor do the words possess exact meanings which can transcend time and place. It is the power relations contained in the whole process of Statementing which are enduring, for it is these which become manifest in the Statementing process. It is through the representations of active social relations which exist in the statutory process of Statementing that power relations come to 'endure when the text stops'.

The whole enterprise of assessing the special needs of children is one in which all the participants, child, parent, teacher, LEA officer and psychologist, are caught in a web of power relations which is generated subject to particular issues of history, power and economics. The process of 'Statementing' thus consists of activities and contains symbols which are subject to political control and variability, 'Political regimes thus conducted a silent war for the control of the symbols and rites of belonging to the human race within their frontiers, not least through their control of the public school system' (Hobsbawm, 1987, p. 106).

Texts and Truths

In this section I place before the reader extracts from professional texts written about James, a boy that I have known for several years now. The words will originally have been written by a professional concerning the pathologized (James) and they have been selected by this author and will be read by you as a reader.

In their original form the words written about James acknowledge no such possible analyses (or dilemmas). In their original form, many of those words written by the professional and read by a reader, will also have purported to convey truths, unequivocal singular truths about the pathologized. Furthermore, many of these words produced by the various professionals will have been regarded by some (different readers) during the years as holding such knowledge (or power) of (over) the pathologized as to justify the making of decisions about the pathologized's life. In this section I suggest that the arguments which form the basis for those decisions may be primarily economic rather than psychological.

In terms of informing my daily practices as a psychologist, an important element of this method is that the initial relationship between the professionals and the pathologized, the seers and the seen, should always be available for analysis. The reader is again invited to consider questions of knowledge itself. For example:

- what can actually be 'known' of the pathologized (James)?
- do the accounts written by the professionals contain that 'knowledge'?
- are the professionals invisible?
- if not, what proportion of the professionals' accounts can be regarded as the professional and what proportion can be regarded as the 'truth' of the pathologized?

Other questions will continually become available, however, for example:

- how does a reader relate to the 'knowledge'?
- is the original 'knowledge' claimed by the professional available to be known by either this author or the reader?
- if 'knowledge' claimed by the professional or the pathologized can be known exactly either by an author or a reader, how can their relationship be accounted for? That the author and the reader should be invisible seems an untenable position.

It is a contention of this chapter that, in producing texts, and by representing them as truths, professionals (for example, psychologists, teachers, social workers and health professionals) engage in social practices which, whilst analyzable in psychological terms, are performed as economic acts. In considering these other (mainly professional) texts, however, the reader is not thus invited to the position that this particular text contains the unified or 'closed' 'truths', either of other texts, or indeed of James. For it is argued here, not that truths cannot exist, but rather that such truths of a person cannot be reduced to, or read simply as, text.

It is a further contention here, however, that there are indeed particular texts which make claims to such knowledge; that there are texts which effectively lay claim to unified truths about people and that these texts are produced by professionals. An argument here is that professional texts are allowed to convey the truths of individuals in ways that do not restrict the extent of their claims to knowledge and power. It is the further contention that, whilst professional texts are not necessarily 'truths', they are of necessity 'texts' and as texts they can be open to rational scientific scrutiny and analysis. The questions of knowledge and ownership which can be a consideration for rational scientific method are here considered vital to the analyses of the pathologizing processes which permeate the following accounts.

I argue that discourse analytic methods continue to hold particular possibilities for conducting such analyses. In many of the texts, therefore, it is not the truths, but the claims to truth which become visible. By making any claims to 'know' any 'truth', however, especially of another, the accounts begin to move beyond the boundaries of a rational scientific analysis upon which their knowledge would seem to be based and towards a metaphysics for which psychoanalytic accounts have often been dismissed. Also, the texts are not reducible to individual authors and are concerned with institutional positions (for example, professional/client) rather than the particular characterizations of specific individuals within those positions.

And now to James.

> *'Thank you for your letter about James with the request that I should see him for his behaviour problems. At clinic on [date] his parents told me that they consider him immature for his age but very bright. They are concerned that he still wets himself and has faecal incontinence from time to time, although he is nearly 4 and has difficulties which have arisen at his nursery school where he has been found at times to be disruptive and his teacher has indicated that he may still have difficulty in starting at school because of this.'*
>
> (correspondence between doctors)

> *'Time is running out, as he is due to start school. He also has other behaviour problems ... but the toilet is the greatest worry.'*
>
> (letter from James's mother, Mrs 'Lee', to an educational psychologist)

> *'premature – 7 weeks – 4lb. 14oz. Stayed in special care for 3 weeks.'*
>
> (notes from first educational psychologist)

> *'James is going to [name of school] in September as Auntie takes the reception class there and wants him under her wing! He will then probably go back to [another school] ... '*
>
> (correspondence between doctors)

> *'During my brief intervention I noted a number of concerns regarding James's*

development and I feel he is a child with a number of difficulties which will become even more apparent now that he has started school ... poor language development ... poor fine and gross motor development ... poor social development. ... Although James can demonstrate knowledge of a number of cognitive skills prerequisite for success in the reception class. ... I feel that he has been taught these by rote and he has developed minimal understanding.'

(letter from first educational psychologist to a doctor)

'James is not fulfilling his potential socially or intellectually. ... He still, however, is unable to work independently and needs one to one attention.'

(re-referral letter from James's headteacher to Educational Psychology Service)

'James is generally functioning within the high average category. However he demonstrates well above average skills in some areas. There are some minor indications of developmental immaturity in terms of gross motor co-ordination and social skills.'

(report written by second educational psychologist)

'Hello Mr Billington' [with air of resignation]
(I asked)'what do you not like in school?'
'I answered that last time; do you want me to give you the same answer?'
[closed his eyes again drawing]
James likes ... 'Shadow Guests' by Joan Aitken, Sleeping Beauty, Snow White
I told him of Christmas Carol and Great Expectations.

(author's notes from discussions with James on his own in school, as third educational psychologist)

'James is to be removed from class for a period of time if his behaviour is disruptive ... should James's behaviour deteriorate then the school will seek an immediate psychological assessment ... '

(letter from school to Mr and Mrs Lee)

'problems with his friends ... one of them annoys him – won't let him pass him on the way to school ... [James said] "he thinks I'm a pain, but I'm not really" '.

(author's notes from discussion with James)

'During this week James's behaviour has deteriorated, so much so that he had to stay in with myself and other teachers so that he could eat his lunch without disturbing others.'

(letter from school to Mr and Mrs Lee)

'*I wish to confirm that you were telephoned and asked to collect James from school following a biting incident.*'

(letter from school to Mr and Mrs Lee)

'*Will chat very well (sometimes too much!) if he is in the mood or it is something he wants to talk about.*'

What do you think your child's special educational needs are?

'*More individual attention to help him with his class work … his sudden displays of immature behaviour are often seen as naughtiness but I don't always feel he realizes what he is doing.*'

How do you think these can be catered for?

'*By extra resources … *'

(parental responses to questionnaire issued by LEA to inform them of parents' views as part of Formal Assessment, 'Statementing' process)

'*I have no alternative but to ask you to collect James each lunch time until further notice.*'

(letter from school to Mr and Mrs Lee)

'*During individual work with James, he often engaged in conversation which contained vocabulary and concepts which were beyond his years … He has an intelligence which is rich with possibilities and he has the potential to have a very successful educational career.*'

(from author's 'Psychological Advice' provided under the 1993 Education Act)

'*This child was assessed by the Special Needs Assessment Panel [date]. It was recommended that I request you arrange a meeting, early in the new term, with the headteacher and the educational psychologist to discuss the type of support necessary to meet James's needs within his current mainstream school.*'

(Internal Memo from the LEA to Head of Learning Support Services)

'*I have seen your report regarding [James]. I wonder if you had thought about this young man in the light of attention deficit disorder.*'

(letter from a doctor to the author)

'*could not conclude what James's problem was … can't label at this point, cannot say he has A.D.D. but he definitely needs one to one support … does James have any obsessive moments?*' (doctor)

> *'school not always the appropriate place and this will depend on level and quality of support'*
>
> (Case Conference notes compiled by a teacher)

> *'We have formally labelled James as having Asperger's Syndrome, that is, high functioning autism.'*
>
> (correspondence between doctors)

> *'this year's been better than previous years ... he's still not able to survive in the classroom without support'* (headteacher)
>
> (author's notes from case review meeting)

As a reader you will now have formed some of your own ideas about James, the pathologized. It is part of the 'method' in this chapter, however, that those ideas will, of course, have been mediated by various professionals and by myself as author. Nevertheless it seems likely that you as reader, on the basis of those mediated texts, will have made some judgements of your own. These may have been about James, or about the textual content provided by the various authors, or perhaps about the merits of the different professional accounts and statements. Again, it is neither the accuracy nor the validity of any of the above accounts which is directly at issue here. Rather it is consideration of the underlying reasons for, and consequences of the whole enterprise of child scrutiny itself, an enterprise in which a host of people spend large portions of their life's work in creating truths about people such as James. This project commands massive human and economic resources.

Now the initial reason given for this economic enterprise seems to be based on a claim by some of the adults that James is in some way 'different' and eventually this leads to the claim that his needs are 'special'. Implicit within that claim is a further claim that the adult involvement will be helpful to James and that it will result in him having his needs met. The reader may notice that James's own evidence (as the pathologized) is not presented directly and identified as such. I would suggest that this is because within the whole process, James's evidence does not possess the power conveyed by either professional or adult accounts and is not considered as essential to the process. Any account of James can usually achieve the status of truth only through the power of an adult voice.

James, clearly, is not considered to have such a knowledge of himself; and yet, he does attempt to lay claim to such self-knowledge on occasions. For example, when James speaks of the boy who is harrassing him he says of him, *'he thinks I'm a pain but I'm not really'*. A point here is that James is not considered to have a knowledge of himself, and this is a view which can be supported by some accounts within developmental psychology, accounts which can be circulated by professionals (for example, the paediatrician and the psychologist) and also by non-professional adults alike.

Now it can be argued that most children are allocated to this position of having no knowledge of themselves, so it remains to be seen why it was that only James in his class at school had the power to command the huge adult investigative enterprise into his 'needs', supported as it was by the discourses of a developmental psychology (see Burman, 1994). Clearly, however, that power was not James's to command. In considering the original referral, it would seem that it was James's parents who had the power to trigger the initial professional activity from their GP. I suggest that although it can appear that it was they who had the power to command the enterprise, however, the situation may have contained other potent elements.

Pathology, Statements and Economic Processes

The opening words in James's file belong to a doctor in correspondence with James's GP – *'Thank you for your letter … that I should see James for his behaviour problems'*. It would seem that James had been taken to their GP by his parents because he was proving difficult to manage within the home. At this point, therefore, by invoking such discourses as 'parents should be able to manage their children', I suggest that Mr and Mrs Lee may have been reacting to a discourse which is primarily social rather than purely psychological. The discourse that parents have a duty to 'manage' their children's behaviour can become a social imperative in certain circumstances under law (and this legal responsibility seems likely to increase). Mr and Mrs Lee's referral, therefore, could be seen as a product of their anxieties regarding the social consequences of 'failing' to manage James, a situation in which they may well have feared the (social) pathology which could ultimately have serious repercussions.

The problem could also be considered to be an economic one, as Mr and Mrs Lee did not appear to command the resources of human labour which would be necessary to manage James without recourse to further social intervention. It may be that if they had had access to such resources, for example within the family or within the local community, the initial referral may not have been necessary. The discourses of developmental psychology are invoked by the various participants from the outset in order that the economic problem can be transformed and relocated within a psychologized pathology. I would suggest that there is a danger of missing economic and social arguments when psychologists (or other professionals) are seduced by the convenience of such individualized and reductionist models of pathology.

I argue further that the economic and social concerns which were active in the initial referral, can be seen to occur throughout the text, at different stages of the process. Indeed, all the first four contributors in James's file had concerns which relate to James's predicted ability to attend school. Again, I suggest that before being tempted to see only James or any pathology, it is important that we see the recurring discourses which touch upon his ability to attend school and that the issues have economic components which can easily be overlooked.

I suggest that one of the reasons for generating the whole assessment process is not to ascertain James's psychological well-being, but to regulate an economic potential – the psychological assessment is used to assess his ability to fulfil the social and economic requirements of school attendance (and may also affect his parents' access to different economic opportunities). The point at which James as an individual is scrutinized in order to assess his availability for inclusion or exclusion from school is crucial. The outcome may in turn lead to his exclusion from other levels of economic activity later in life. It is not necessarily medical or psychological questions which generate and permeate the process, therefore, but rather social and economic issues:

> *'he may have difficulty starting school'* (a doctor)
> *'time is running out, as he is due to start in school'* (Mrs Lee)
> *'James is going to [name of school] in September as Auntie takes the reception class there and wants him under her wing!'* (a doctor)
> *'I feel that he is a child with a number of difficulties which will become even more apparent now he has started school.'* (the first educational psychologist)

It is social and economic arguments which permeate these (individual) concerns and it is through these arguments that an individual's capacity to be contained by (included within) a school is assessed. Now although the psychologist would often resist such analyses in favour of the individual pathology, these social and economic arguments (although denied as factors within the pathologizing of an individual) are considered to be of such importance that vast amounts of money are spent in order to allow the education system to police with this statutory force. The statutes are required, not necessarily to meet the needs of children, but because schools, populated as they are by children between the ages of 5 and 16, are a culturally and historically specific means of controlling the labour market:

> In your book *Deterring Democracy*, you argue that the one fundamental goal of any well-crafted indoctrination program is to direct attention elsewhere away from effective power. Do you think that this is also one of the goals of schooling?
> Yes. A good example of this is the role of corporations in American life. I'm sure if you investigated schools, or for that matter universities, you would find virtually no attention paid to this subject. The questions of how corporations came into existence in their current state is a major topic of American history, but you only find out about it in specialist studies ... But it's obviously the central question. Somebody like Adam Smith would have picked that out as the central topic to discuss, but there's essentially nothing about it.
> (McLean and Chomsky, in McLean, 1995, pp. 138–139)

I argue here that training for professionals who work with children has indeed directed attention 'elsewhere away from effective power'. Perhaps, therefore, although it is still tempting to look at James and his individual difficulties, we need to know more of the processes which, firstly, would exercise some control over his social and economic life by regulating his education. Secondly, however, as James fails to comply with the social and economic demands of school life in a satisfactory manner, we need to keep sight of the attempts which are then made to exclude him from access to certain aspects of social and economic life, which here initially lie in his fixed exclusions from school. These processes are eventually managed through the psychological assessment procedures.

The economic aspects and consequences of the whole investigative process can become easier to see once the request for 'Formal Assessment' is made by the school. It is then that the school's inability to manage James's behaviour sets the next part of the exclusion process in motion. For the school begins to consider that their economic resources are insufficient to manage James, and that successful management of his behaviours can only be achieved through an unequal distribution of their own labours which would be to the detriment of the other children – *'James's behaviour has deteriorated, so much so, that he had to stay in with myself and other teachers'* (teacher). The issue of resources often resurfaces during the accounts: *'How do you think [James's special educational needs] can be catered for?'* (LEA questionnaire) *'By extra resources'* (parents). *'[H]e definitely needs one to one support'* (doctor).

Now the law states that it is James's needs which are to be considered, not the school's needs, but how is this the case? The school's request actually hinges, not upon James's educational and psychological needs but rather on the following. Firstly, he is seen to consume resources within the school greater than those to which he is entitled within a supposedly egalitarian system of economic distribution. Secondly, this unequal distribution is claimed to have a detrimental effect upon the economic resources available to the others in the school. Thirdly, the school wishes either to gain extra resources or else they want him to leave. This is the point frequently at issue within a request for a statutory assessment of a child's needs. The school, therefore, may be allowed to exclude James from their community not necessarily because James has 'special' needs but because of their own economic needs. The process of meeting these economic needs within this story moved on to a different stage following the decision of the local authority assessment panel meeting:

> *'I request you arrange a meeting, early in the new term, with the headteacher and the educational psychologist to discuss the type of support necessary to meet James's needs within his current mainstream school.'*
>
> (LEA officer)

The decision, therefore, is an economic one, as both the request for, and allocation of, support are a means of controlling financial possibilities.

The Decision

Now we can bear in mind again here, that the assessment panel who are making the decision about the allocation of resources to meet James's needs are, of course, merely other readers of the evidence. Such panels can consist of LEA inspectors or administrators, specialist teachers, educational psychologists, headteachers and paediatricians, many of whom will not have met the children concerned. The evidence upon which their decision is based is contained in those accounts from the earlier parts of this chapter. As readers, the decisions made by the panel will be based on the 'truths' represented by the various writers – professionals. In reaching their decision they will have followed a different route from you as reader for they did not have to take account of the additional mediator, this author. Nevertheless, as readers their decision was made based on the claims to truth of the various writers, the professionals, claims which I would suggest are at least questionable.

Such assessment panels throughout England and Wales deal with tens of thousands of children every year and the time available for them to read all the various pieces of information, digest and discuss at meetings will often be limited. There are certain constraints which affect the quality of decision-making, therefore, related to the amount of the panel's time which is deemed to be economic in reaching a decision. The consequences of their decisions, meanwhile, depend upon the resources which are available to them for distribution. Attempts are made, therefore, to make the decision process easier, by constructing various criteria, for example. Often, those criteria are based upon information provided by the psychologist such as that provided by psychometric tests of ability and attainment.

There are many instances of children being removed (excluded) from their current school and placed in another because of the allocation by the psychologist of a pathology which is based on such statistical truths. For example, in Chapter 2 Gary had been excluded originally in one area for having 'learning difficulties'. In James's case, however, I was not the only professional to make the claim that he was of above average ability and that his attainments were also good. This information about his learning capabilities, however, as with Gary, was not going to provide a suitable location for the pathology.

One doctor, mindful perhaps of continuing parental concerns, not least regarding the school's propensity to continue to tolerate James's presence, attempted initially to locate James's pathology within his behaviour, considering the application of the label 'ADD' (p. 63). Having 'failed' with 'ADD', however, the subsequent attempt was more convincing as considerable professional power was employed in order to allocate another pathology, diagnosing James as having 'Asperger's Syndrome'. I suggest that in considering the various accounts, it is this individual pathologization which can mark James out for special consideration and which makes a convincing claim upon special (economic) resources.

The investigation complete, the only decision to make was the scale of the resources to be allocated and this depended largely on a deal being struck between the school and the LEA. But where was James in all this? It would almost be easy to forget him as the crucial arguments seemed to be:

- What was the minimum figure the school would accept from the LEA in order not to exclude James?
- Could the LEA meet the cost of the school's demands?
- Would it be cheaper for the LEA to place James elsewhere? In other words, would it be more economical to permit James's exclusion?
- What professional evidence could be utilized to justify those economic decisions?

Ultimately, there would appear to be direct links between the allocation of a specific pathology, the allocation of an economic resource and the exclusion of individual children. The overseers of the available resources need professional accounts of children's lives which both facilitate the economic enterprise and which are also structured according to economic demands. I would argue, however, that there are truths which can be overlooked in this enterprise. For in being dazzled by the reductionist pathology of 'Asperger's Syndrome' which is allocated to James, we can easily become separated from:

- James;
- our own representations of James;
- our own knowledge of the economic processes which demand such pathologies.

Endpiece

In Chapters 2 and 3, the reader was provided with different accounts of the processes of pathologization and the social segregation which can ensue. In Chapters 4 and 5, I have continued this approach, setting before the reader various representations of Mary and James, both my own and those of other professionals. It has been through consideration of language itself, however, in particular by theorizing its capacity for truth and/or representation, that I have sought to explore further those social practices and processes that actively separate and exclude children on the basis of stigmatized differences.

Now I suggest that the five outcomes of psychopathologization mentioned earlier (pp. 22 and 32) are again a useful guide in assessing the processes and outcomes for the children who have been scrutinized by psychology and represented by its language in Chapters 4 and 5. In respect of the first possibility, changing schools, neither Mary nor James (nor Gary in Chapter 2) were actually removed (excluded) from their schools. I would argue that, for Mary and James (and also Gary), exclusion had been a likely outcome, but that it had been resisted in different ways. For example, in all three cases, personal commitment would seem to have been important, whether by parents, teachers, LEA officers or myself. It should be noted, however, that in none of the cases would the personal commitment of the child subject have been sufficient to resist the exclusion.

Resistances had also been economic, but this too was far from simple; for, in the cases of Gary and Mary, the Local Education Authority chose to offer the schools no financial reward for continuing to accept them, and actively refused to move them on account of its own limited resources. By contrast, however, I suspect that it had only been the allocation of extra money to pay for a classroom assistant that had enabled James to stay at his school.

Given that economic factors can be seen to operate in the separating and excluding of children in such ways, it is important that I now begin to construct analyses of their activities.

Suggestions for Further Reading

John Berger's trilogy *Pig Earth* preserves some insightful ways of viewing the links between language and society and provides starting points for considering changes in community action.

Erica Burman's (1994) *Deconstructing Developmental Psychology* again de-stabilizes some of the claims that are made for otherwise 'a priori' stories of child development, suggesting issues and questions which can lead to change.

Psychology, Discourse Practice (Burman et al., 1996a) provides an array of diverse contexts in which discourse analytic work can be applied, for example, in traditional domains such as education and health as well as in arenas such as advertising or issues such as parenting.

6 Memory, History and the Division Of Labour

> Memory is life. It is always carried by groups of living people, and therefore it is in permanent evolution. It is subject to the dialectics of remembering and forgetting, unaware of its successive deformations, open to all kinds of use and manipulation. Sometimes it remains latent for long periods, then suddenly revives. History is the always incomplete and problematic reconstruction of what is no longer there. Memory always belongs to our time and forms a lived bond with the eternal present; history is a representation of the past.
>
> (Nora in Hobsbawm [1984], 1987)

The past is used as the organizing theme of this chapter in order to allow, not only reflection upon some of our contemporary activities but also consideration of questions of economic knowledge. I use reconstructions from my own childhood as well as examples from literature to argue that children can possess sophisticated economic knowledge, whilst I also invoke different historical accounts in order to highlight the changing concepts of children and work. I consider three kinds of evidence to support the hypotheses that economic knowledge permeates our social relationships, that it can be known at an early age, and that it lives in psychological practices:

- *representations of my childhood;*
- *the story of Pip and Estella from* Great Expectations;
- *estimates of comparative wealth between myself as psychologist, and the subjects of my professional practices.*

'It's All About Money Isn't It?'

You may well have heard this said, perhaps thought it, or even said it. Whether as a teacher, perhaps coping with a lack of resources in the classroom, or as a social worker trying to provide help to young people in situations which seem to offer prospects of anything but care, or else as a health worker delivering therapies devised primarily to deal with long waiting lists, perhaps it might just have crossed your mind that money does play an important part in our working lives. Perhaps it may have crossed your mind too should you be a hard-pressed administrator in any of the agencies, under fire, from practitioners, fund-holders or else the general public. I suggest, therefore, that we are committing a serious scientific error whenever we fail to take into account economic factors as crucial variables both in the lives of the individual children with whom we work as well as in the professional practices and relationships in which we engage.

The allocation of resources is certainly an important aspect of the Formal Assessment or Statementing processes in which thousands of child professionals are engaged in the English education system and this is known to many of the parents I meet. In order to understand the circumstances in which children's needs are assessed, are either met or unmet, therefore, it is important to keep in mind the ways in which the economic nature of the processes fuel the professional and decision-making activities which affect (individual) children's lives.

The modes of scrutinizing, pathologizing and individualizing children's differences are so prevalent, however, that special acts are required in order that economic activity remains visible as an active variable in professional practices. This chapter thus aims to be one such special act, capable of providing resistances against some of the prevailing discourses which more usually contrive to locate specific problems totally within individual children. It strives instead to keep available alternative means for knowing children which take more account of the social and economic circumstances which affect their lives. In order to understand the nature of economic activity, however, we need a historicized account which can take into account the changes in social organization which have affected people's lives during the last two to three hundred years in 'Western' economies.

The changing nature of economic circumstances during the eighteenth and nineteenth centuries was recognized at the time by many political economists and reformers (for example, Adam Smith, Robert Owen amongst many others) as affecting all contemporary human activity and production, however defined – perhaps working or writing. Whilst the new economic conditions sweeping Britain during the Industrial Revolution began to transform the nature of human activity it can further be argued that the nature of knowledge itself changed as it became subject to the powers of ownership: 'knowledge purchased, in the same manner as shoes or stockings, from those whose business it is to make up and prepare for the market that particular species of goods' (Smith, in Scott, 1937, p. 345). Through exposing the ways in which changes in knowledge reflected changes in social and economic productive relations, Smith thus made possible a critique of intellectual production as part of his overall analysis of labour.

Subject to the conditions of economic production, knowledge and reason too became commodities, with properties which were later assigned to professional domains such as psychology or education within the expanding economic processes – 'the massive advance of the world economy of industrial capitalism, of the social order it represented, of the ideas and beliefs which seemed to legitimise and ratify it: in reason, science, progress and liberalism' (Hobsbawm, 1975, p. 15).

Just as the discourses and practices of pathology were to emerge and take different forms during recent centuries, so too did perceptions of children and childhood. The social sciences, psychology or education, for example, appeared later in the nineteenth century generating more discrete forms of knowledge about the 'true' nature of people and children, and simultaneously searching for any deviance from the evolving social norms. I argue, however, that given the scale of their enterprise, the spectacular success within the market place of social sciences such as psychology or education is balanced just as spectacularly by their lack of success if we consider their inability to unearth uncontestable, universal human truths. And yet, they are a home to activities in which such truths form the 'common sense' of daily professional practices.

In order to contemplate any form of deviation from the normalizing imperative which permeates a capitalized reason (the eponymous 'differences') I suggest that materialist, economic accounts of history can provide helpful starting points. There is a particular historical need to preserve such means of analyzing the processes in which differences come to be 'discovered', especially since 'we can no longer guarantee that history will provide the right outcome' (Hobsbawm, 1987, p. 340).

In this chapter, therefore, I search for a psychological language, method and practice which can keep alive (economic and political) memories (analyses) of a past in order that they can live as knowledge in, and of, a present. I thus invoke 'Vygotsky's insistence on the primacy of the search for method, specifically on the necessity of discovering the proper unit of study' (Newman and Holzman, 1993, p. 22). The memories of the past which I represent in the next two chapters as contemporary knowledge are concepts which are again taken one from each of the last three centuries respectively, and to which the reader is introduced here in brief – the division of labour, alienation and projective identification:

- the division of labour is a consequence of the new industrialized conditions for trade and economics during the last three hundred years. It refers to the social distribution of different activities and their confinement within particular specialisms. For example, whilst I claim some specialism as a psychologist, I neither grow the food I eat nor make the clothes I wear, for these have become the specialist preserve of others within the market place;
- alienation is a complex term which can be used in different ways (see Williams, 1976) but whilst I imply a usual sense of 'making external to oneself', I assume its link to, and inter-dependency with social, historical processes;
- projective identification is the term associated in particular with the works of the psychoanalyst Melanie Klein which refers to 'the ejection into the outside world of something which the subject refuses in himself [*sic*]' (Laplanche and Pontalis, 1988, p. 356).

Memories of Childhood and Economic Organization

Memories of my first friend are vivid. The sense memory of her, I am sure, has been re-worked many times, but although it is resistant to my attempts at an accurate written realization, I have memories which still hold something of the quality of how it was like to be with her. I remember, for example, her confidence, the straightforward approach to life which she seemed to possess, and which I found irresistible. I remember also some of those times we spent together at the front of the house, she bossy, vivacious, always challenging, whilst I seemed relatively passive, playful and watchful.

However, there are two other sets of memories which remain with me, for although I can't remember meeting Anne's parents, I do remember their house, and I do remember knowing that her family was different in some way. Other than the house, specific artefacts or objects in this case are impossible to recall, but the set of memories which knew of Anne's exalted family station in life relative to my own are still alive in me. Another set of memories surround my feelings of loss when she and her family moved away.

Now all of this is, of course, unremarkable, even though the memories are now over forty years old, for we all have such memories. What seems more remarkable now, however, is the unremarkable way in which I knew that Anne carried a certain material wealth, the value of which was almost tangible (although details elude me, I knew it was greater than the wealth we possessed). Anne, of course, was a child-hood friend, but what puzzles me is the way in which I always seemed to have known of her wealth and expectations. This is especially so since I have neither seen, nor heard of, Anne or her family since I was 3 years old.

One of the first books I can ever remember reading was, appropriately, or perhaps inevitably in this case, *Great Expectations* (Dickens [1860–1], 1993). I write 'inevitably' as the book struck such a chord in me possibly in part because of those earlier events during infancy with which I could draw a simple parallel between, on the one hand, the relationship between myself and Anne, and on the other hand the initial relationship outlined by Dickens between Pip and Estella. What is not obvious, however, is the way in which I (and therefore presumably other children), and together with Pip and Estella, without obvious instruction, could know the quality and materiality of both wealth and feeling so early in life.

Just as I had known material 'truths' at the age of 3, so Dickens attributed Pip with economic knowledge as a young boy. The first description of the place where Pip lived, for example, 'Joe's forge adjoined our house, which was a *wooden* house, as many of the dwellings in our country were' (Dickens, 1993, p. 19) contrasts with his first observation of Miss Havisham's, 'Within a quarter of an hour we came to Miss Havisham's house, which was of old *brick*' (p. 57).

These passages seem to me similar in several respects. They both serve as intro-ductions to people and their property; they both give life to the subject who is immediately attributed with (the power of) possession; they both convey, not only the materiality of the possession, but also a material sense of the possession's value; and finally, there is the ever-presence of the story-teller.

As story-tellers, therefore, I share with Dickens the attribution of another, younger part of ourselves with a knowledge of economic truths, not as neat, defin-able units, but as unities which depend for their life on the characteristics of the social relationship in which we both found ourselves. For Pip, his observations of relative material wealth were umbilically connected both to Joe Gargery and to Miss Havisham. In Miss Havisham's case Pip would have made his relationship initially with the material presence of the house (just as readers we do); it is a presence which Pip nevertheless knew immediately to belong to Miss Havisham. In other words, it is not only the material objects which are present, but the material value of those objects, the power of which can only assume its significance within the social exchange of owner and non-owner. For Pip's memories are, amongst other things, of owners and possessions, the knowledge of which exists as part of the social relationship, 'what exists ... is not men [*sic*] but social relations' (Seve, 1978, p. 70).

In my own memories, wherever I can re-present an object from the past in the foreground of the present, for example an old radio in the back room, it is visibly and otherwise sensorily supported by the presence and social exchange of others. The people and the economic memory trace are inseparable and strong enough to insist on preservation. So it is that my own history can reveal a relatively sophisticated knowledge of material, social and economic relationships, all acquired before I reached school age. There are many other memories of a personal history of social relationships in which the understanding of some of the meanings and values of economic exchange were known to me, not as theoretical constructs, but as the material fabric of life, as the houses, the furniture, the toys and above all the social relationships. So it is that I have always lived with, and have always seemed to have an understanding of economic knowledge. I argue that the children whom we meet in professional practice will also possess such knowledge or knowing.

Economics in Practice

Some years ago now, taking a half-hour break from writing to enjoy the blistering July sun, I sat in the small back yard, looked up at the house and suddenly realized that in my reverie I was giving my economic antennae more freedom. How many home visits had I made during the last year? What could I remember of the wealth which was made material in those houses? Would that wealth have communicated to me an economic value more or less than my own? Now surely, if my work as a psychologist was immune to economics, or else if the professional expertise on offer was somehow economically neutral, there would be at least two possible outcomes. Firstly, I would not be able to make any distinction between our respective economic circumstances. Secondly, since I live in a relatively mixed area of a city and in a house valued in a middle band council tax, C, the sample of houses visited would appear to be a random one, with a curve implying a normal distribution between those houses which possessed greater wealth than my own and those which possessed less.

This exercise of including issues of material wealth (mine and others) as part of professional practices could be transformed into a supposedly complex analysis. However, I kept it simple. I first compiled the list of names and moved down the list making instant estimates,[1] reacting to my immediate and not knowingly mediated judgements. These were the figures which were 'computed' on first 'impression':

Total home visits	Greater or equal wealth	Less wealth	No wealth
26	1	18	7 (in care)

Note: Figures taken during a 12-month period several years ago

I argue that those 'impressions' of mine of economic wealth are active and at work inside my professional practices as a psychologist. As such I suggest that it would be unscientific *not* to consider such information as a crucial variable in any analyses I conduct, for example of a child's individual differences. The figures themselves look so convincing, but whilst it would be possible to construct a tighter hypothesis, to demand greater precision would necessitate losing sight of my original concern which was the complex permeability, transportability and immediacy of the economic unity.

If I could make economic judgements at the age of 3, however, how is it possible for me to remain 'stupid' (after Sinason, 1992) to that knowledge now? The further consideration of course, is not merely my own stupidity, but by implication the stupidity of the children and families with whom I work, who it is also assumed have neither the ability, nor the inclination, to possess an economic knowledge. I argue, on the contrary, that economic relationships are present everyday in my social interactions with children and their parents, and that they are known not only to me but both to the parents and also to their children.

Such economic knowledge is not conveyed simplistically but it is conveyed in many complex material forms which include language. Interestingly, however, the language I employ with the subjects of my psychological practices will usually attempt to sidestep the economic dimension. It is almost bizarre, unreal, that the issues which may possibly have an enormous significance in determining my involvement in a case (for example, money, unemployment) are the very issues which I rarely mention. Whilst it is those questions which I never ask, however, they may be uppermost both in my mind (for example, my reluctance to take a drink from Mrs Smith in Chapter 2) and in the minds of those on the receiving end of my questions. These questions may be hard to answer or even contemplate but they include, for example, 'how is the rent to be paid ... the clothes to be paid for ... how will I pay the fuel bills?'

New Economics – New Children

'In the 1860's a new word entered the economic and political vocabulary of the world: "capitalism"' (Hobsbawm, 1975, p. 13). It was during the nineteenth century that our contemporary economic conditions were becoming established in many countries, 'In this era industrial capitalism became a genuine world economy and the globe was therefore transformed from a geographical expression into a constant operational reality. History from now on became world history' (Hobsbawm, 1962, p. 63).

The earlier analyses of Adam Smith can be recognized as seminal in the development of political economics and his theories indicate that the power and machinery of capital, although not then global, could be sensed from the middle years of the eighteenth century onwards. Indeed, the unique points of history through which Smith lived enabled him to have knowledge of a world with, and also without, capital and his representations of the new economics allow us to see that he could make a crucial distinction 'between the reason for exchange and the measurement of that which is exchangeable' (Foucault, 1970, p. 224).

It is now over two hundred years since Smith began to articulate the new, complex forms of economic exchange and in so doing he also revealed processes which, he concluded, affected individual lives and their social conditions in fundamental ways. Smith's theses, whilst essentially economic, and despite being written over two centuries ago, have a contemporary social relevance, 'The theoretical economics of the *Wealth of Nations* rests upon two assumptions of a broadly sociological character: first, that man [*sic*] is found in the social state, and second, that man will be found within a particular type of social structure wherever the exchange economy prevails.' (Skinner in Smith [1776], 1970, p. 14).

One of Smith's most perceptive contributions concerned the changing nature of human production and therefore our social relations within the emerging economic processes, for he 'unearths labour, that is toil and tire, the working day that at once patterns and uses up a man's life' (Foucault, 1970, p. 225). Smith's analyses soon became subject to modifications, refinements and additions, by Ricardo and Marx for example, but I argue here that those essential economic conditions existing within the new relationships, and which Smith articulated as formative in people's lives, still pertain. For just as history lives in people's lives and accounts today, so do those economic forces, despite the obscuring of such powers through, and in, agencies such as psychology and education (see Chomsky in McLean, 1995).

Smith identified four 'stages' of economic development in human evolution – hunting, pasturage, farming and commerce (Smith [1776], 1970, p. 13) but, in particular, he recognized the different lives that people were experiencing as a consequence of the changes in economic organization. Smith saw the different ways of living which were being born within the new form of commercial activity, initially because what was to become known as capitalism was still in its infancy and also because its new industrialized conditions for living were, as yet, localized rather than truly global. At this time there still existed alternative ways of living outside the new economics.

Even forty years after the *Wealth of Nations*, however, the newness and particular nature of living in a world ordered according to capital could still be discerned, for not only did reformers and educationalists such as Robert Owen describe the new economic and social conditions, they also indicated the ways in which they lived inside human experience, 'A change in the conditions of production effects an essential change in the human producers; the Industrial Revolution was such a change, and produced what was virtually a new human being' (Owen [1815], in Williams, 1987, p. 26). Owen's conclusion can now, nearly two hundred years later, be considered a psychological hypothesis, but it is a hypothesis which gives a more general analytical leverage upon current dilemmas concerning the opposition between the individual and the social. History here, in Owen's analysis of the way in which individual human experience is umbilically connected to the social and economic, allows us to reflect upon the present, in which such analyses can often lie hidden, for example within, and by, many of the practices of modern psychology.

Through his original historical and economic analysis Smith enabled us to see the fissure between individual people and the conditions of the capitalized social order and thus exposed the character of a social and economic dislocation which continues in our modern experience and analysis and which was later to be recognized by Marx.[2]

Both detected the fundamental difference and made visible the changing consequences for individual experience which might now be represented as 'psychological'. It would be unhistorical to look back on the Middle Ages, for example, as some halcyon era, however, and the historical method in this chapter is merely a way of keeping alive certain stories about ourselves in the present.

The Division of Labour – a Matter of Life and Death

One outcome of industrialization has been the development of mechanisms/technologies which have been designed to regulate, to bring order to, the available workforce. One important economic (and psychological) consequence of such regulation and enfranchisement is the necessity to divide people into a seemingly limitless number of 'populations' (see Chapters 3 and 7; also Duden, 1992) and there has developed a constant need to measure people in relation to one another and put them into categories. Often, the effect of this exercise has been either to exclude certain categories of people permanently from the wealth-creating process, or else mark them as being available to provide extra sources of cheap labour should there be a shortage or else a need for another kind of economic adjustment.

The historian Hobsbawm provides us with one example of a large 'population' or 'group' which has constantly been singled out in this economic process of regulation, enfranchisement and exclusion during the last two hundred years. In so doing he also indicated the consequences when he described nineteenth-century industrialization as, 'a process which tended to extrude women, and particularly married women, from the economy officially defined as such, namely that in which only those who received an individual cash income counted as 'occupied'. ... It produced a certain masculinization of what economics regarded as labour' (Hobsbawm, 1987, p. 199).

This is one of the many consequences which relate to what is a very particular understanding of a specialized 'work', for activity which is paid work and which is directly linked to the generation of capital has assumed particular characteristics and special status, a manifestation of a unique power to recreate one's own life. In Britain today, however, millions of people still do not have that status; in particular, many women and black people, homeless people, increasing numbers of men, old people, young people, those who are defined as having 'special needs' of one form or another; millions of people are currently disenfranchised from achieving the desired economic status of 'worker' by regulatory means in support of economic control.

Work can seem to have become the ultimate measure of value within society and therefore the power to command work has become the ultimate human activity. Ultimate, yes, because the human potentials suggested within the capitalized system of economic organization, which are the lifeforce behind the achievement of Western reason,[3] are linked to processes which attempt to transcend that reason. For we have tantalizingly before us now representations of an infinite humanity which find parallels in economic processes, 'The characteristic feature of capitalist accumulation is precisely that it appears to have no limit. The natural frontiers of Standard Oil, the Deutsche Bank, the De Beers Diamond Corporation were at the end of the universe, or rather at the limits of their capacity to expand' (Hobsbawm, 1987, p. 318).

Such unreason is frequently either ignored or unseen, however, and the prevailing, public view is that an economy based on the accumulation of capital will 'not only create a world of suitably distributed material plenty, but of ever-growing enlightenment, reason and human opportunity, an advance of the sciences and arts, in brief a world of continuous and accelerating material and moral progress' (Hobsbawm, 1975, p. 13). As individuals we experience economic and social processes which have the capacity to trick us into believing in the possibility of never-ending progress and plenty. However, within the process we can experience fragmentations in a correspondingly never-ending series of oppositions, an example of which is the opposition between work and non-work which indeed become as life and death. This is no singular dilemma, however, for within those of us who work, the production of our own life and its subsequent expropriation by economic imperatives, can appear as life and death also. To be unemployed or unemployable meanwhile is an undesirable state in which we become diseased in relation to those who work whilst the fear of unemployment, however, can be as death both to those who work and to those who don't.

Human experience is now mediated by such oppositions and power relations which are subject to the laws of a particular kind of economic production; the search for meaning becomes even more intense under such conditions. Neither that search nor the polarities are new of course, but the possibility exists that all such oppositions, meanings and values are being consumed by a voracious global economics and that a knowledge of them outside that mediation will eventually no longer be possible.

It is within the particular terms and conditions of this economic process that, not only do we experience our separation from others, but we also experience the fragmentation within ourselves (NB alienation). Now it is in addressing such fragmentations of experience that psychology has flourished and for which it has purported to provide a symbolic language; for example, psychoanalysis attempts to provide an account of experience which can attend to questions relating to individual identity and attachment. But such questions have only been raised within that process of fragmentation which has permeated economic organization during the last few centuries. The ways in which individuals experience dislocation, either from one another or else from themselves within their own work, are generated by processes which now organize all our lives and work and I connect them here to what Adam Smith termed 'the division of labour': 'The division of labour ... occasions, in every art, a proportionate increase of the productive powers of the population. The separation of the different trades and employments from one another seems to have taken place in consequence of this advantage' (Smith [1776], 1970, p. 110).

There had been an increase in specialist trades during the Middle Ages but for the most part, people would spend much of their lives surrounded by material objects which had been hewn out of a localized social fabric. Following the Renaissance, however, and the growing economic organization and industrialization, there had occurred an exponential growth in the quantity of manufactures. The features of the new markets and industries included the expansion of specialized forms of work together with a corresponding increase in the number of manufactured objects in people's lives for which they could have no social grasp or understanding. Increasingly, people use objects in their lives which present as 'fantastic', as we have little understanding of, or explanation for, their conception or manufacture in much the same way as now I have very little grasp of the immensity of the human endeavours which are before me as I write; for example, just how does the print appear on the VDU screen?

Smith suggested that 'Labour, therefore, is the real measure of the exchangeable value of all commodities' (Smith [1776], 1970, p. 133) and that this value has become universal through the increasing specialization of our activities. He could also foresee some of the possible human consequences of the division of labour. For example, he not only predicted an increase in the quantity and specialization of work but he also warned as to consequences, 'The division of labour ... might lead to "mental mutilation" through narrowing the range of activities undertaken by individuals' (ibid., p. 81) The consequences for the individual, which can now become located within the domain of the psychological as well as the economic, are thus considerable.

Smith also analyzed that, whilst the value of things could now be contained and measured by the quantities of labour which they could command, the value of those acts of labour did not necessarily correspond with the quantities of labour originally expended. Quality and quantity had become visible (Marx [1844], 1977, p. 107) and divisible in a fundamental act of separation which, I would argue, has become omnipresent in our social relations. In this way, individuals will experience a dislocation which may well be experienced, in particular, by those who have been excluded from 'work' activities. This separation and loss can be experienced by all of us in different ways, including:

- separation from, and loss of, the product of our labours;
- separation from, and loss of, other producers;
- separation from, and loss of, parts of ourselves.

The individual can experience these processes in different ways, but at whatever level, it will be known in experience as material separation and material loss. Psychology is one of the agencies through which we can come to know this unreason within economic, social relations, as reason.

Economic Reflexivity

It is at this point that it becomes possible again to see the emerging themes of separation and fragmentation within the various specialized forms of work which have developed into professional practices, for example within domains of knowledge such as education or psychology. The economic nature of the work generated in such domains could be described as follows. In our work with children, professionals within education and psychology make available a range of theoretical principles which, through processes of revelation and discovery, expose individual child subjects to forms of scrutiny in which either the individuals seem to declare themselves for selection or else are declared by psychological expertise and psychological discourses (see Parker, 1992; Burman and Parker, 1993). I argue that the means of identification, however, are sustained by social, economic processes which have the power to define that which should be identified in accordance with their own particular needs and laws. Once the methods of individual scrutiny and identification have been codified and established, it becomes a relatively easy matter for other (economic) forces to devise new social practices which are either more or less liberal as the (economic) situation demands. A question arises, therefore, of whether it is possible for us to escape these economic processes in our work, for example, as educationalists, social workers or psychologists?

During months and years of writing, I have not knowingly experienced any element of compulsion in the activity and although I always find the work difficult, it seems to be an activity into which I enter freely. However, if I refer to as work those acts which I will perform tomorrow as an educational psychologist, then what I am doing now appears as something different, perhaps non-work. And yet the performance of writing this book is long, tiring, exhausting activity; it must be work, surely?

The activity tomorrow, by contrast, performed as an educational psychologist, could present itself as work for it is the money earned in performance of that activity which provides for direct and essential physical needs, and makes possible my eating, drinking and sleeping. As such there could be an umbilical connection between that work and my life, for it is through the performance of such work that the necessity of my life can be sustained economically. Given different circumstances, however, I would not go to work tomorrow for somehow that specialized work required of me appears to me as not me, and any umbilical connection appears to be, at the very least, twisted. For I know that often, I experience a separation in the performance of the work, both from the work itself and also from myself within the activity.

The dilemma is not between the opposition of work and non-work, however, nor is the opposition to be found necessarily in the economic necessity or otherwise of the work. I would argue that one opposition is that which I know between myself and my activity, within the performance of the individual (and psychological) acts, wherever enacted.

In considering as economic production both kinds of specialized psychological activity (firstly, writing – secondly, working with children), neither activity appears to be directly linked to the propagation of capital. Whilst I do receive money for my performance of psychological acts upon children, their families and their teachers, I do not appear to be a producer of capital within those acts. In writing articles and theses, meanwhile, I have received no money at all, and in fact the reverse can apply, for it is I who have often had to make payments. Psychology, therefore, it would appear, can take different economic positions which seem unconnected to economic production. I would argue, however, that this is but a fantasy and that the system of productive relations presents as universal, and further, that the means exists now of quantifying the value of any activity according to (potential) wage-labour-power (see Marx [1857–8], 1977).

For the wage-labour of a professional, in my case as an educational psychologist, allows the individual to transform their work activity into the means of commanding other varying amounts of other labour-power. Given the need for economic survival and given that those powers of subsistence are directly related to forms of economic exchange, all social acts can be linked to an economic labour-power, whether inside or outside my life as a psychologist. The apparent 'free' service I offer at the point of delivery is subject to those same social and economic relations and therefore whatever psychology I perform constitutes an economic act.

All the acts which I perform in the name of psychology, therefore, are material acts which live in the world of social and economic production and exchange. Any subsequent denial I might make, or any act performed in which the social and economic become invisible, are as flights from reality. Economic life has to be considered inside any supposedly psychological question. It is not this that is so remarkable, however, for what is more remarkable is that our economic life and our psychological life could ever have been separated in the first place – a most basic division of labour.

Endpiece

This section, therefore, has once again attempted to work its way towards the method in which can be found the 'proper unit of study'; for to remove either ourselves or else remove the economic nature of our work from what we do as professionals working with children appears as cruel deceit. It is important, therefore, to acknowledge that the economic survival of many professionals who work with children relies on our ability to participate in the regulation of the economic potential of the children with whom we meet. Whenever the economic dimension becomes invisible in our work, it is not that the truth and the individual experience described is false; rather, that they must be incomplete. For when as a professional, a psychologist, I meet with a child, there is a fundamental economic relationship which, in its simplest form, can be represented as follows – I receive money, the child does not.

Suggestions for Further Reading

Adam Smith's *Wealth of Nations* was written at a point in history (late eighteenth century) when, perhaps, it was easier to conceive of a world before the capitalization of all markets.
Karl Marx understood Smith's concepts of the 'division of labour' and 'surplus value' but wrote during the middle years of the nineteenth century at a point when it was easier to see the ways in which capitalized industrialization had affected people's lives. In particular, the *Economic and Philosophical Manuscripts* (orig. 1844) and *Grundrisse* (orig. 1857) explore links between the philosophical, the political and the economic.
Eric Hobsbawm is a twentieth-century historian whose materialist approach to the history of the last three hundred years provides scholarly yet accessible accounts (in four volumes; see References).

7   Alienation or Pathology?

> The biggest danger, that of losing oneself, can pass off in the world
> quietly as if it were nothing; every other loss, an arm, a leg, five dollars
> ... is bound to be noticed.
>
> (Kierkegaard, 1989, pp. 62–63)

*The concepts of alienation and projective identification are used in this chapter to
consider aspects of human experience and objectification. It is suggested that alienation relates not only to economic processes, but can be seen to relate to processes
which are usually regarded now to be 'psychological'. The link between these
processes and those processes contained within the domain of psychoanalytic object-
relations generally and projective identification specifically are considered.*

ALIENATION

Alienation provides a means of informing us of the living history in which the recent
modes of material production continue to exert their influence upon our own
contemporary psychological experiences, 'Lukacs has asserted ... that alienation is
the most promising of all subjects' (Mandel and Novack, 1970, p. 5). The extent to
which alienation either is, or is not, psychological, however, in accordance with the
division of labour, can only effectively be challenged through the authority vested in
people who are regarded as having psychological knowledge – psychologists
or psychiatrists, for example. I suggest, however, that the ultimate arbiter of the
acceptability of alienation within a psychologized text, however, does not necessarily
depend on the strength of its claims to 'truth' but rather on its potential utilitarian
value in performing economic acts. Alienation as psychological experience will thus
come to be either accepted or rejected according to any of the following three
principles:

* it possesses a potential for generating capital – economic/cultural;
* it possesses the potential to perform regulatory acts in support of economic
  processes;

- it possesses the potential to offer resistances which in turn can further stimulate the economic processes.

The work of the modern psychopathologist[1] demands, effectively, that we measure people's behaviours and potentials against one another. The results of this measurement may well be crucial for the individual who is measured, leading either to their acceptance or else their exclusion from wealth-making activity and its associated benefits of power and status. Through the performance of (social) acts and discourses, the modern psychopathologist is required to make available, not the individual, but only the behaviour of the individual within the confines of inter-personal power relations which are organized according to economic interests. It becomes one of the most important tasks for professionals employed to work with children, therefore, that they can:

- access children's failure to achieve those particular behaviours which are deemed acceptable by economic processes;
- represent those failures as individual;
- allow the economic circumstances which make possible or likely that failure, to remain hidden.

The argument for the inclusion of alienation here, therefore, is that it offers a potential to resist non-science, by holding in view the interests and power of the economic processes which lie hidden inside contemporary practices and discourses with individual children.

Now the concept of alienation manages to provide a site in which to consider what has become a fundamental separation within Western society: the apparent dichotomy between the individual and the social (there do often still seem to be only those two possibilities). Freud's supposedly psychological theses, of course, articulated ways of penetrating the individual, whilst Marx's supposedly economic theses informed the social. The important sense of the social in Freud, a potential which was rarely highlighted in his clinical practices, has only been developed by later analysts (for example in the work of group analysts such as Bion, 1962). The social implications of the structures for individual experience and inter-personal relations which Freud postulated have also generally only been realized by his successors (for example, 'projective identification', Klein [1948], 1988).

The experience of alienation is so elusive as theory because it lives inside a separation between the economic and the psychological. Whilst connections between alienation as economic and alienation as psychological are rare, however, 'Alienation is a focal point from which to view human beings and hence to speak of them, one which stresses the fact of segmentation or practical breakdown of the inter-connected elements in their definition' (Ollmann, 1971, p. 133). Many writers have recognized the 'psychological' within Marx's economic theories[2] but the concept of alienation itself was specifically related to psychology, in particular psychoanalysis, by Robert Hinshelwood (1983, 1985, 1996). On the whole, however, whilst alienation has been viewed primarily as an economic term, here I challenge that division of labour by arguing that alienation can permeate the materiality of what would otherwise remain separate, either as economics or as psychology but as (social) experience.

Alienation as experience, not merely as concept or philosophy, provides a view of the individual and their behaviour as inseparable from the specific economic conditions in which they find themselves. I suggest, therefore, that alienation is a part of a dialectical process in which it is both a product and a producer of contemporary social and economic life. Alienation is alive in our (social) consciousness and alive in our (material) psychology and, therefore, in my work as an educational psychologist. It might live also both in the writing and in the reading of this book. Woven so strongly into the concept of alienation, however, is the notion of the social that it can lead to a further position in which it can be argued that an individual cannot be analyzed as such, for it will only be inside social relations that the individual can come to be known, 'it is the relation which is the actual foundation of things' (Seve, 1978, p. 263). It is my argument that it is within those relations that alienation can be found.

Alienation – Philosophy and Experience

Much of Western philosophy since Descartes has been drawn to dualism in whatever form, mind/body, subject/object, nature/nurture, female/male, black/white (see Ryle, 1949). The dialectical methods suggested by the nineteenth-century philosopher, Hegel, however, allow movements and relations beyond such dualisms. He hypothesized a dialectical method of mind in which there existed a relationship between things in which the original (the thesis) and its opposite (the antithesis or negation of the thesis) could be unified (in the synthesis or negation of the negation). That process of subject, the illusory object and the overcoming of the illusion is Hegel's dialectical process of mind, mind estranged and mind coming back to itself. Hegel called the illusion of the object, *Entfremdung* – 'estranged' – but sometimes he called it *Entäusserung* – 'alienated'.[3]

'Alienation is one of the most difficult words in the language. Quite apart from its common usage in general contexts, it carries specific but disputed meanings in a range of disciplines from social and economic theory to philosophy and psychology' (Williams, 1976). Williams traces two main strands of meaning in the evolution of the word within the English language, '(i) an action of estranging or state of estrangement: normally in relation to a cutting-off or being cut off from God ... (ii) action of transferring the ownership of anything to another'. Meszvaros' definition of a Marxian alienation in a society organized according to the demands of capitalized exchange is also helpful:

a) man [*sic*] is alienated from nature
b) he is alienated from himself (from his activity)
c) from his 'species-being' (from his being as a member of the human species)
d) man is alienated from man (from other men).

(Meszvaros, 1970, p. 14)

Alienation is not only possible within a society organized according to the demands of capital, however, and indeed, 'The isolated individual ... estranged from other people and even from his own deepest self and emotions, is a familiar character in all branches of contemporary writing' (Mandel and Novack, 1970, p. 5). Such social isolation, estrangement or alienation is, of course, not just a recent phenomenon, for 'some of the principal themes of modern theories of alienation appeared in European thought, in one form or another, many centuries ago' (Meszvaros, 1970, p. 27). It is, however, the particular quality of alienation which has occurred within the changed economic circumstances during the last two hundred years in particular which distinguishes it from other forms of objectification. I argue that alienation can occur within contemporary economic exchange, as each individual relinquishes part of themselves in their work (in acts which can be both voluntary and involuntary). This relinquished part can then be transformed into capital value which is owned by another. It is inside this interaction in which alienation lives.[4]

There is a 'conceptual line of demarcation between LABOUR as "*Lebensäusserung*" (manifestation of life) and as "*Lebensentäusserung*" (alienation of life). LABOUR is "*Lebensentäusserung*" when "I wish to work in order to live, in order to produce a means to living", i.e. my activity is forced upon me "by an external necessity" instead of being motivated by a need corresponding to an "inner necessity" ' (Meszvaros, 1970, p. 91). The experience within my labours as an educational psychologist, therefore, might now often be seen as '*Lebensentäusserung*', alienated labour, or 'alienation of life'. Despite of, or perhaps even because of, its internal contradictions, however, it is now possible to see this book-work as '*Lebensäusserung*', work which is being performed as a consequence of a motivation which feels like an 'inner necessity'.

Alienation from ...

It is part of the structure of alienation that there is always the sense of 'alienation from', a sense of individual separation from something, someone, or indeed oneself, as other. This implies a relation and causality which, whilst not necessarily equal, nevertheless leaves the elements of relation and their causality as equally valid questions, and thus more available for analysis.

Alienation thus has the potential to position the 'other' as a more central concern, and has the potential to attribute any other with the status not merely of an object but with that of another living subject. The other (living) subject implied in 'alienation from' assumes an importance greater than that which can be made available by other analytical means, for example, through some forms of psychoanalytic projective identification. For I would argue that alienation also contains within it a more vividly social character and potential as against the (usually) individualized nature of the object presented in projective identification. The object within psychoanalysis, although valid, is usually attributed with life only in respect of the life force exhibited by the initial subject.

By contrast, within a materialist alienation, the (social) action of the object is, by implication, an active force which itself has the power to prompt, or perhaps even demand, the life of the original subject, and as such should be considered as another subject with its own validity. The 'other' within alienation, therefore, becomes not an object but another (social) subject, and can thus be afforded more status when analyzing issues of experience and identity within the individual first subject. Alienation, I argue, makes visible a huge mass of other possible subjects which interact with the individual subject. Whilst allowing for individual capacities to act upon their environment, alienation not only allows the environment to act upon the individual, it posits this as fundamental within the dialectical process.

Once the truly reciprocal and dialectical nature of the relationship between the individual and the society of other subjects is highlighted, it becomes possible to conceive of a different kind of concern. Instead of the focus being on the nature of a particular individual, the attention can turn to the reasons for the privileging of one kind of gaze (on one individual, for example) over another kind of gaze (on the society of other subjects). Indeed, it also then becomes possible to analyze the particular nature of the separation of the individual from the social world which is itself a product of a most fundamental division of labour. The powers of reason can thus enable us to address the powers within reason which select and privilege its subject matter.

I suggest that these are material processes that occur between, and inside, relations. These relations are not merely inter-personal but are also intra-personal and inter-subject. They are born of processes in which all relationships, between (and inside) individuals, become infused with the knowledge of economic production. It is the nature of those material processes which, I argue, indicates that in our economic exchanges and social relationships, something of ourselves can be lost and expropriated against our wishes and can be accumulated as value by the other (although not without our, at least, partial or subconscious, material knowledge). It is in this giving up of part of ourselves to another, either unknowingly or unwillingly, through our work, that alienation begins to assume its unique (economic and psychological) form.

It is that process within the current economic order that operates in our relationships, within ourselves, between individual people and between individual people and their life-products. The economic processes are such that we can find the 'me' in others and the 'not me' within ourselves. The interactive nature of this material process is such that as, increasingly, we have acted upon all our environments, nothing appears unaltered by the economic circumstances in which we circulate. We thus become both lost and found in everything for in the material objects which surround us we find those parts of ourselves which we would not have given, and the more we produce, the more of ourselves we lose, 'the poorer we become'. In that exchange we can also begin to find those parts of others which they too may not have wished to have given, and which we may also have wished not to receive.

In this section, therefore, I have argued that alienation *is* a separation, one which can be brought into existence through the divisions of labour between our economic and our psychological experience. I suggest that a focus on alienation holds the potential to generate different analyses of relations. For as method it might provide sites for considering various relationships, the individual and the social, the economic and the psychological, through utilizing dialectical and material processes.

I argue that acknowledging and focusing upon alienation might enable professionals to:

- resist the divisions in human experience generated by professional practices;
- avoid searching, automatically, for individual positions;
- avoid positioning as central, questions of (individual) pathology;
- provide a way of representing experience which necessitates the taking into account of the various economic relations;
- provide a resistance to those powers of regulation which seek to pathologize (individual) behaviour;
- view the relationship between individual and social pathology.

PSYCHOANALYTIC RELOCATIONS

> We live in a psychoanalytic culture, and it is as much a pre-condition for psychology that it expresses and legitimizes psychoanalytic thought as it expels and refuses home to psychoanalytic theorists.
>
> (Parker, 1997, p. 159)

Institutions such as schools and Local Education Authorities have little cause currently to seek overtly psychoanalytic representations of children. This may be because psychoanalytic readings within current practices are more able to resist a censorial approach to behaviour, although this resistance will vary according to the particular cultural, historical and political circumstances. Currently, however, psychoanalysis (at least in Anglo-US contexts) would appear to make possible a greater commitment to the interests of the individual subject of analysis. It would certainly appear to be more committed to acknowledging and scrutinizing the analysts themselves (e.g. through developing more reflexive practices and through concepts such as 'counter-transference'). My argument, however, does not preclude the possibilities for oppression which psychoanalysis may come to offer in different cultural and political circumstances.

In practice, my employer (the LEA) often accepts representations of children which are infused by psychoanalytic readings; for example, those readings which acknowledge the complexity of emotional lives and unconscious processes such as 'trauma', 'bereavement', 'attachment'. Such readings, at one time the property of psychoanalysis, were by stealth purloined by a mainstream psychology which at the same time has been reluctant to admit to their theoretical origins. These readings of our emotional lives have, of course, now passed through psychology and have been subsumed into a cultural 'common sense' but I suspect that it would be unacceptable were I to conduct individual assessments according to explicit psychoanalytic methodology to the exclusion of all else.

Regulatory authorities demand easy access to theories and practices which can justify acts of government. LEAs and schools, therefore, are attracted to more pragmatic and less speculative forms of psychological knowledge and representation than that currently offered by psychoanalysis. A further reason for this (apart from those discussed earlier in the book) may be that a function of these educational institutions is to keep hidden that which psychoanalysis might reveal, 'It is not psychology that is involved in psychoanalysis: but precisely an experience of unreason that it has been psychology's meaning in the modern world, to mask' (Foucault, 1967, p. 198).

The school and the LEA are some of the institutional forms in which are negotiated the boundaries of reason and unreason. For example, Statements of Special Need produced by LEAs supposedly respond to the needs of individual children. Built upon the Enlightenment's foundations of science and state, however, the institutional forms employed in their production only respond to needs which can be deemed reasonable, for schools and LEAs are institutions which are based upon reason and statistics ('science of state' – Rose, 1989). Any individual need deemed unreasonable, therefore, is unlikely to be met. In order to consider how unreason might be contained within the confines of a particular, 'pathologized' category of social disability which is policed by, amongst others, schools and LEAs, I will be referring in Chapter 9 to children with whom I have worked who have each been allocated a specific pathology – 'autism'.

I will be arguing that the effect of a pathology such as autism is to re-present for scrutiny the apparent non-human unreason of the person described as autistic, which is characterized by their behaviour. I argue here, however, that it is only by engaging in speculation upon the apparent unreason evidenced by the pathologized individual, that we might come to know more of their reason and more of our own unreason. In order to do this I will employ psychoanalytic readings. Now whilst various justifications are often invoked to oppose psychoanalytic readings within mainstream psychology, I tend to agree with the psychoanalyst, Jacques Lacan when he wrote, 'The radical heteronomy that Freud's discovery shows within man [*sic*] can never again be covered over without whatever is used to hide it being profoundly dishonest' (Lacan, 1977, p. 172).

Psychoanalysis has thus provided us with a creative means of speculating upon human action. Whilst it originated as a model for articulating human, intra-relational experience, certain psychoanalytic approaches have begun to take into account the significance of human, *inter*-relations. The theory of object-relations provides an example of how some practitioners have attempted to organize their thinking and work in this area.

'Object-relations are the subject's mode of relation to the world – the entire complex outcomes of a particular organization of the personality, of an apprehension of objects that is to some extent or other phantasied, and of certain special types of defence' (Laplanche and Pontalis, 1988, p. 277). NB: an 'object' in psychoanalysis has a special (non-pejorative) sense whilst 'relations' imply inter-relationship.

Although often regarded as committed to an innatist, asocial model, I argue that

Melanie Klein's work on 'object-relations' begins to imply a model for human inter-activity existing from birth, 'I have often expressed the view that object-relations exist from the beginning of life ... that the relation to the first object implies its introjection and projection, and thus from the beginning object-relations are moulded by an interaction between internal and external objects and situations.' (Klein [1946], 1988, p. 2). Now Klein's 'objects' can appear somewhat static and non-dynamic but her analysis above at least begins to cast doubt on both the inevitability and the viability of a completely autonomous, individual psychological life. Klein's theory of 'object-relations' relies upon her definition of the twin concepts of introjection and projection, which are as follows:

> Introjection means that the outer world, its impact, the situations the infant lives through, and the objects he [*sic*] encounters, are not only experienced as external but are taken into the self and become part of his inner life ...
>
> Projection, which goes on simultaneously, implies that there is a capacity to attribute to other people around him feelings of various kinds, predominantly love and hate.
>
> ([1959], 1988, p. 250)

Now it is not my intention to engage in a detailed critique of Kleinian analysis. It is the living, the activity which is implied in her model which is interesting, for, as is the case with any concept or theory, here of introjection and projection, there will be a residue which cannot be contained by any fossilized enunciation of its properties. I am more interested in the movement which is implicit in Klein's model, the oscilla-tion between introjection and projection. In Klein's model this movement from the individual person to the outside and vice-versa begins at birth.[5]

I am less interested here in the specifics of a particular theory, however, for 'object-relations' is only one such theory which begins to acknowledge movement in the picture. It is theories of processes, however, theories of movement, which seem to elude even the most sensitive and process-minded psychologized representation and I argue that any claims to accuracy made by a particular theory or representation can too easily become as individual photographs, attempting to 'freeze' individualized moments and experiences in time and space.

Indeed, Western culture seems fascinated by frozen, atomized 'photographs', mistaking pictures of individual characteristics, contextually isolated, for life itself. It is as if the movement of (living) processes is just too difficult for us to theorize. I suggest that in failing to acknowledge processes and by choosing instead the *cate-gory*, we deny the vitality of human experience. The models of experience which psychology creates tend to exacerbate this atomization by pursuing concepts of concretized human differences. It is in such ways that we lose sight of, lose the feel of, and also lose touch with both the movement and also the 'sameness' of people, the nature of the inter-relatedness between ourselves and others. Through constantly attempting to 'freeze the frame', we construct fragmented snapshots which unerringly omit an 'other', and effectively restrict the possibility of change which may obey more natural, dynamic laws of movement.

I suggest that it is models which are more able to embrace movement–space–time, which might prove resistant to psychology's current project of highlighting supposedly frozen, individualized and pathologized differences. It is the processes, the movement and the activity which are implicit in Klein's model which indicate the possibility of constant interaction and inter-dependence, for example, between an 'I' and an 'other', however represented.

There would appear to be clear distinctions between whatever I can regard as an 'I' and whatever you might regard as your 'I'. But is this such a problem? Well, psychology would seem to think so, given the vast amounts of human labour which is expended in search of individual differences. Indeed, I argue that psychology has been charged with conducting that search for individual differences and that it constantly generates new technologies, scientific projects, many of which are used to scrutinize and highlight fragmented scraps of information in the form of individualized and pathologized differences.

A more psychoanalytic reading of these processes, however, may open up new possibilities. Klein's proposal for a psychoanalytic representation of an individual's interaction with the world concerned the activities of 'projection' and 'introjection' of 'good' and 'bad' objects, which in turn lead to the consequent splitting of 'love' and 'hate' (e.g. Klein [1946], 1988, p. 2, and [1959], p. 250). A Kleinian perspective might suggest that our concern with individual, pathologized differences is due to the ways in which relationships between individual 'I's become invested with, or even infected by, 'bad' elements. It is within such processes that Klein believes that individual 'I's are formed, 'The intrinsic connection between identification and introjection … identification as a sequel to introjection is a part of normal development' ([1955], 1988, p. 141).

Through an intense effort to gaze upon a frozen foreground of the individual, however, I suggest that we might fail to notice the *movement* between the elements. A foreground can only be seen *in-relation-to* a shifting background, and any frozen gaze upon an individual will fail to access a more dynamic understanding of their movement in the world.

Fragmented Experience

I suggest that there are other ways of viewing these processes and relations. For example, I have suggested that figures from the eighteenth and nineteenth centuries (Adam Smith, Robert Owen and Karl Marx) were recognizing that the conditions in which human beings were living their lives were changing as a consequence of economic and social factors. Ollman (1971) believed that considering 'alienation' provides us with a (different), 'focal point from which to view human beings and hence to speak of them, one which stresses the fact of segmentation or practical breakdown of the inter-connected elements in their definition' (p. 325).

The British psychoanalyst, Hinshelwood, has more recently explored connections between 'alienation' as a psychological process and Kleinian concepts of projective identification, 'Marx described an unmistakable and very concrete form of projective identification … he called it 'alienation'. Alienation is a psychological process that inserts man [*sic*] into particular relationships with his social environment.

Projective identification is the primitive forerunner of all social relationships' (Hinshelwood, 1983, pp. 221–224).

Now 'object-relations' psychoanalysis argues that our identities emerge from a series of introjections and projections, basically a process in which we are constantly *taking 'objects' in*, and *putting 'objects' outside* ourselves. In this way we can lose parts of ourselves ('good' and 'bad') as we place them in other people through projection and take in, perhaps unwanted, parts of other people and 'objects' through introjection. I argue (after Hinshelwood) that the concept of 'alienation' too suggests processes in which people can lose part of themselves, both through their labours and also within the products of their labours (and simultaneously become poorer, perhaps economically and psychologically). The concept of alienation also suggests processes in which people may have to 'take in' unwanted material products of others.

Both conceptually and practically, 'alienation' and 'projective identification' attempt to articulate those processes in which we form our (social) identity. They both theorize, too, the ways in which people can begin to experience difficulties and can begin to question more frantically the nature of their own identities. 'Alienation' and 'projective identification' would provide the basis for narratives of fragmentation, as our own atomized characteristics and those of others become separated yet impossible to disentangle.

I suggest that there now exists in our contemporary economic world a multitude of possible identities with which we have to cope. For example, concepts of 'opportunity' offer us the possibility of some*thing* other and we are bombarded by cultural representations of how we might seek to change ourselves in adverts etc. We are now presented with choices, therefore, even as to whom we should be as we are beset by an array of choices that can challenge and confuse our identities. At such times, as part of the process of alienated experience, we might find that we need to cling on, not necessarily to ourselves, but to various introjects which permeate our culture. One specific reference point, or discourse, by which we endeavour to fix the position of our identity and which permeates many others is the transient, yet durable, psychologized concept of 'normal' and 'abnormal'. I argue that the contemporary discourse of the 'normal' human being is one that is encouraged by psychology. I also argue that we are all affected by this discursive introject, and that we can become mesmerized by its ability to permeate many cultural discourses, thus affecting the continual flow and exchange of both 'good' and 'bad' objects.

Hinshelwood was not the first to speculate upon the psychological repercussions upon the individual of the modern processes of economic production. Hinshelwood's particular perspective, however, does allow us to see a process in which, through our creation of more and more material objects through industrial production, we have more and more opportunities both to lose more parts of ourselves and also to gain more parts of others in the continual processes of projection and introjection. Such material products are designed to affect our symbolic lives and we are thus forming our personalities in a process of mass projective identification, which Hinshelwood argues *is* alienation, 'We can postulate that capitalist society brings out in the individual personality, the potential for excessive projective identification (alienation). In turn projective identification spurs on the form of capitalist society' (Hinshelwood, 1983, p. 225).

Needing to Label

In Chapter 3 I explored one particular set of arguments concerning the pathologization of children which depended on the concepts of a psychological normality and *ab*normality. I suggest that these concepts/activities have become psychologized reference points that interact with our individual identities and experiences. Discourses of difference and abnormality have, increasingly, been policed by psychology.

However, as global economic production continues to expand, so does the range of possible introjects. Hinshelwood postulated that the ever-expanding nature of economic production would result in 'excessive projective identification'. Should this be the case, then, we might expect that increasing numbers of people might begin to experience an increasing number of possibilities which are connected to issues of identity and personality and we might hypothesize, therefore, that the pathologizing tendency which invades questions of identity will expand similarly.

It is important to remember, however, that regulatory processes contain resistances. One current resistance, for example, can be found in the calls for inclusion. Some LEAs are looking to respond to such discourses by rationalizing their SEN provision, not necessarily on ethical or scientific grounds, but on the basis of economic concerns, for it can be cheaper to educate children in mainstream schools than in 'special schools' in which there are more staff per child. Despite this particular economic imperative, however, and despite oft-stated policies of 'inclusion', LEAs continue to segregate children as efforts to close special schools can meet with counter-resistance from various sources, for example, parents who view the special provision as better for their child than a mainstream school, or else from professionals who see removal of the child as being a solution to an individualized problem. History suggests that the industry of child regulation will continue to expand, although increasingly subtle measures may well be needed in order to prove acceptable to a broad liberal consensus.

One current area of 'growth' in Special Educational Needs is 'autism'. Now such syndromes are relatively new categories which have been 'discovered' during the last fifty years or so and they have all been classified by the American Psychiatric Association's 'Diagnostic and Statistical Manual' (DSM-IVR) as being 'disorders' of one kind or another (whether developmental or personality often seems largely irrelevant to the policing agencies).

In one way, such diagnoses may seem due to scientific innovation but Hinshelwood had forecast that a growth in the number of borderline personality disorders would be likely to increase as a consequence, not as a result, of any outstanding scientific *progress*, but because of the expanding nature of our economic production. He explained it thus, again attempting to address the link between human activity and the nature of our social conditions for living, 'The possibility that projective identification/alienation is enhanced as a defence mechanism by the increasing development of society, would go towards explaining the noticed change in symptomatology from hysterical conversion towards borderline personality disorders over the last one hundred years' (1983, p. 225).

Now the growth in recognition of disorders in children such as autism and

Asperger's Syndrome, and most recently AD/HD constitutes evidence of this change in 'symptomatology' and it is a change which I see in my work as an educational psychologist. The change in the patterns of pathologization (but not necessarily the processes) is evidenced by the structural changes in school placement currently being tentatively proposed by different LEAs (for example, new units/schools). There seem to be increasing numbers of children whom I am called to assess who have already been diagnosed (or who soon will be) as having one particular form of specific disorder/pathology. Such categories act as reference points. I hesitate to call them 'fixed' reference points, for it seems likely that psychology will be able to 'discover' an unlimited supply of new 'disorders' which will supersede these current categories. It is not the individual category which is 'fixed', despite its appearance, but the stream of pathologization.

Endpiece

Now I argue that the connection between projective identification and alienation that Hinshelwood describes casts doubt upon the origins and nature of individual, psychologized pathologies. I suggest that the expansion in the number of objects which individuals introject and project may be proportional to the expansion in the number of material artefacts and symbols that we produce. Children are born into a world of more and more stimuli, more and more 'good' and 'bad' objects, both to take in and to expel: 'Although in accordance with the general Kleinian position, the urgency behind mental activity is pictured as deriving from instinctual drive processes ... the social world in which the child is embedded has a crucial mediating function which in turn is causal of the condition of the child's internal world. ... Sociality thus enters into the child literally with the mother's milk' (Frosh, 1989).

The dynamic of the inter-activity can too easily be lost in representation, but there have been exponential increases in the stimuli (either 'good' or 'bad' objects) with which children have to cope, demanding of them more and more separating, more and more losing. It is quite possible that the sheer volume of introjects with which a child has to cope when working with new technologies such as television, digital media services and computers effectively bombards a child with cultural information which demands more and more psychological activities in the form of symbolization.

Children thus enter into a world which has its processes of pathologizing and excluding ready for them.

So just whose pathology is it?

Suggestions for Further Reading

Marx's *Economic and Philosophical Manuscripts* illuminate the concept of 'alienation' and also provide informative links to the works of Hegel and Feuerbach.

Many of Klein's more accessible and later works can be found in the collection, *Envy and Gratitude* (1988).

Robert Hinshelwood is a source, not only of contemporary Kleinian thinking (e.g. *Clinical Klein*) but also of links between the domains of psychology and politics (see various articles).

8 Tales from the Autistic Spectrum

> The more one dips in [to the soul, the mind, the character of a person],
> the more one finds what is common and familiar to all.
>
> (Tolstoy [1892], in Christian, 1978)

Autism is just one of many categories around which are organized particular kinds of human stories. In this chapter, I explore ways of representing three cases in which the categorization of autistic spectrum disorders has been allocated. I have known both James and Peter for several years now, whilst Donna Williams has received a diagnosis of autism and has since written several books about her life. In the first part of the chapter, I take this opportunity to experiment with textual evidence in ways which are designed to provoke professional reflection. In the second part, I suggest certain psychoanalytic reference points which practitioners might consider when working with those children described as autistic.

REPRESENTING CASES

> The characters of course never start literally *ab initio*; they plunge in
> *medias res*, the beginnings of their story already made for them by what
> and who has gone before.
>
> (MacIntyre, 1981, p. 215)

In earlier chapters I have considered the cases of Gary, Mary and James and looked at the processes in which they were allocated a particular pathology. In Chapter 7, however, I utilized other analyses in an attempt to reposition the pathologizing tendency. The analyses which I proposed suggest that the processes of pathologization would themselves have an impact on Gary, Mary and James, and render them vulnerable, as any subsequent social interactions would become saturated with introjections and projections related to the specific characteristics of their allotted pathology. In this way, I argue here that one of the consequences of allocating a fixed pathology is that a child will then be forced to 'swallow' back (Sinason,

1992) or 'introject', their own attributed pathology, whether 'autism', 'behaviour difficulties' or 'Asperger's Syndrome' in their relations with adults.

Now in this book I have argued that those attributed pathologies, of Gary, Mary and James (the pathologized) have been circulated by various professionals as acts of government. In such circumstances claims to knowledge become crucial for the individual. But could a 'pathologized' become a professional and if so, how could this be done? The next section contains Donna's words, and although now she is a professional (writer) she first wrote these words when she was still just a 'pathologized'. Later in this section, I will write as a professional about two 'pathologized' children – James and Peter – but they will not be called upon to provide their own accounts, as professionals, for example.

I invite you to read successively, extracts of text selected by me which aim to represent the kinds of juxtapositions I encountered in the experiences of my daily practice. Firstly, I provide words which were originally written by 'experts' (professionals). Such words often claim some authority over, and generalizability to many pathologized children. Without comment by me, the reader is then provided with words which were written by Donna – originally as a pathologized – but, of course which are words now selected by me as author of this book. I also provide the reader with alternative ways of representing certain events which occurred during the course of my assessments of Peter and James (James received his diagnosis of Asperger's Syndrome, p. 64, whilst Peter had received a diagnosis of 'severe autism' prior to my involvement). As reader you are now left to construct interpretations and stories prior to the further representations which I make in the second part of the Chapter.

Expert Voice

1   Marked impairments in the use of multiple, non-verbal behaviours such as eye-to-eye gaze, facial expression, body postures and gestures to regulate social interaction ...
2   failure to develop peer relationships appropriate to developmental level ...
3   a lack of spontaneous seeking to share enjoyment, interests or achievements ...
4   lack of social or emotional reciprocity.

(DSM IV, 1994)

Donna

The more I became aware of the world around me, the more I became afraid. ... I was frightened. ... My world was full of imaginary friends. They were far more magical, reliable, predictable and real than other children. ... Other people did not understand the symbolism I used. ... Trish cuddled me. ... I was terrified. It seemed tears were welling up from a part of me long buried and forgotten. ... I always paid for closeness with fear.

(Donna Williams, 1992) (see also Billington, 1997 and Billington, 2000a)

Peter

… has severe autism
A week after I had first watched Peter, I stood in the class some metres from him
       I tried to hide my remembrance of him
            He committed no such lie
Peter looked at me
       Smiled and waved
… has severe autism

After another minute he put his milk down
       Walked unnecessarily close to me and pinched my tummy
… has severe autism

One fine day in the schoolyard
       Standing by the tree, swinging,
            Knowing the girl was near
                Seemed enough for Peter
… has severe autism

            (Taken from my report to the LEA under the 1993
               Education Act and also field notes)

James

Or 'Four Meetings In Space'

1.   Eyes I

Sitting alone, children surrounding
Staring at the classroom board
Watching me watching …
Now with me, finding tests easy
Staring at the clock
Watching me watching …
Moving outside, his mother pressing the wall
Passing
Their eyes just once
Meeting, flashing
Fearing
Watching one another watching …

2.   Words I

Staring at the wallmap
'Wales looks like it nearly goes on forever', he said
Questions
– who are your friends?
Silence, he said

Choices
– yes, I'd rather not answer, no
'I'd rather not answer', he said
Suggestions
– you can ask me
'How many friends have you?'

3. *Eyes II*

The pencil in his mouth
Fifteen minutes to move around the desk
The sharp lead sweeping closer to my eyes

4. *Words II*

'Would you like to see my things?', he asked
The huge drawer in the old chest will barely
open … books … crammed
'How many things have you?', he asked.

(Taken from the report to the LEA under the 1993
Education Act and field notes made during visits to school and home)

As reader you will have views on those representations and you will have formed opinions about Donna, Peter and James. It is not my intention to anticipate your own particular interests here, however, for, at this moment, your views upon the characters rely inevitably on voices and characters which have been shaped by me as author of this text. The characters, therefore, if unities at all, are but secondary unities, 'subordinated to the first [me] and incorporated as one of its components' (Bakhtin, 1984, p. 187).

Prior to any further representations of Donna, James and Peter, I reiterate a position taken in this book, for although I cannot disclaim authority (for indeed I do have authority in my work as an educational psychologist) I can at least restrict the claims of my knowledge/authority by declaring it to be largely speculative. I would, however, claim that such speculation is evidence necessarily, neither of a lack of knowledge nor of incompetence for, 'Achievement … [is] capable of being in uncertainties, mysteries, doubts, without any irritable reaching after fact and reason' (Keats, in Bion, 1970, p. 125).

This, however, is in marked contrast to the usual authoritative position adopted by professionals, for example teachers and psychologists, who are called upon increasingly to provide precise, absolute knowledge about children. Professional insecurities, however, cannot be hidden by any 'irritable reaching' after a mode of knowing which searches for such supposed certainties in clinical categories, for example of 'autism' and 'Asperger's Syndrome'. The processes which underpin this kind of science, which is a reductive science of human categorization and simplified differences, can too easily be suffused with the authoritative and the punitive and also reluctant to admit the inherently speculative nature of its own scientific project. In this chapter, therefore, I will speculate with some authority, not upon a particular pathology, nor upon particular differences, but upon common experiences of separating, knowing and learning which, I argue, we might share with one another and share also with Donna, James and Peter.

The discourses in this section, then, move around considerations of the similarities between 'normal' and 'abnormal' human beings; the similarities between us, as 'normal' and those from whom we might commonly be thought to be separate, the 'abnormal'. The questions which are implicit throughout the book, however, can be active again in this section, for '*are some readings better than others?*' and, '*on what basis should we select one reading as opposed to another?*'

DISCOURSES ON MIND – FEELING, THINKING AND LEARNING

> The most striking refrain running through autistic people's accounts of their inner experience is the word 'fear'.
>
> (Boucher, 1996, p. 87)

Feelings

Rarely, either in my graduate education or else in post-graduate training, was the importance of fear in children's experience addressed with any conviction. Indeed, rarely was it even mentioned. There was always a lot of 'behaviour', 'learning' and 'testing' but I struggle to recollect any reference to 'fear'. Indeed, in being trained to work with children who had various problems it usually seemed to be presumed that accounts of their difficulties were completely unrelated to any feelings they might have, let alone any 'fear' which they might experience (or indeed which the professional might experience). Further impressions from professional training were that, since as professionals we had achieved selection for the respective course, we were all basically decent people and that, somehow, all the children with whom we would have to work could be expected to like us too. Whilst children's fear has rarely been represented, that a child would have anything to 'fear' from us as teachers or psychologists can be an even more remote concept. In this chapter, I argue that any understanding which as professionals we might have of a child's difficulties may well be dependent on our ability to understand that child's experience of fear.

In work with individual children, there have also been many whose means of objecting to my approach will have been restricted as they will not have been capable of actually saying 'no' or 'go away'. A lack of verbal response, however, can at its worst be construed either as a tacit approval of the activity or that a child may not have any valid feelings about my presence, whether they be good or bad. Sometimes there can be a leap in my professional logic as a lack of language can somehow come to be evidence either of a lack of feeling or, incredibly, actual consent to my activities.

Mainstream twentieth-century education and psychology seem to be more at ease with children's 'behaviour' than with their 'feelings' and I would argue that many current practices, in my case as an educational psychologist, can often pay scant regard to the feelings of the children with whom we work, in particular at those times when a child may be vulnerable. Usually, children do co-operate with me, but I suspect they do so sometimes in the knowledge that failure so to do (particularly in a statutory assessment situation) might often be to their disadvantage, as any such failure to co-operate could be seen as further proof of their 'difficulties', their transgression. Even if a child could express themselves through language, therefore, they may voice any objections at their peril.

Now the main definitions of autistic characteristics (p. 96) make no reference to the feelings likely to be experienced by the autistic person. Instead, the words which the experts often use to define autistic characteristics – 'abnormal', 'obsessive', 'sameness', 'rigidity', 'stereotypy', 'inflexibility', 'emotionally unresponsive' – would seem to imply that the person under scrutiny is almost non-human, certainly 'abnormal', and conceivably also devoid of thought or feeling. The supposed non-feeling/thought of the autistic person, however, can be implied by some experts who, in the process, it might be said, declare their own thoughts and feelings only too clearly. For the negative, almost pejorative tone of the words often used to describe autism would suggest neither neutrality nor objectivity (see also Billington, 2000 and 2000a).

I am struck by their chosen words as 'signifiers', (p. 47) and I suggest that these words might share a common 'signified'. A common 'signified', I suggest, is not the scientific proof of 'autism', however, but the processes and the power of governments, of social and economic pathologization. The words of the experts, therefore, should not be mistaken for a scientific, or even precise proof of a specific pathology or category. I am reminded of my reaction at the moment the doctor used the words 'Asperger's Syndrome' to 'formally label James' (p. 64). In neither instance have I been impressed by the precision or the clarity of the science on offer, but I have been struck, forcibly, by the power conveyed by such speech acts. In James's case, this indeed was the single sentence for which 'it is necessary to tell a life story' (Berger, 1989).

Professional Descriptions

To what extent is the attack which can be conveyed by professional descriptions attributable either to social and economic processes, or to a scientific consensus upon autism? Or else to what extent is it attributable to the individual 'expert' perpetrators? 'Alienation' and 'projective identification' again provide interesting analytical models with which to address such questions, for example, which might also keep in view the economic circumstances which generate the social processes.

For one of the most likely outcomes of being diagnosed as autistic, I suggest, is the likely restriction upon the individual's wealth-making potential. Such an outcome should not be thought insignificant for it is crucial to know outcomes in order to understand the nature of the activities from which they have resulted, 'In many cases of difficult choice the outcome cannot be foreseen with any certainty ... the outcome determines what has been done' (Nagel, 1979, p. 77). Children described as autistic, therefore, may be victims, not of a psychological 'disorder' but of an economic process. Professionals might ask themselves whether the child's long-term future well-being would be best served with or without allocation of a specific pathology.

Kleinian-based theories of object-relations, however, could well view such pathologies from a different vantage point. For example, we could turn the analytic gaze upon the actual words of the experts, and we might conclude that the words chosen by the experts to describe autistic people might be considered somewhat aggressive. In addressing this same point, Parker suggests that in a 'critical' psychology, researchers, for example, should 'Work with instead of suppressing, what psychoanalytic writers call the counter-transferential investments of the researcher in the phenomena under investigation', (Parker, 1997, p. 166). Any psychologist or expert might consider the feelings and processes which lie inside their own words, and in so doing might see a movement which is more akin to projective identification. The process might be one in which, for example, particular 'bad objects' or feelings could be assigned to particular individuals. Sinason's suggestion that pathologized individuals, here those described as autistic, have to swallow the knowledge of their particular pathologization in such situations and interactions with professionals would again seem at the very least to offer one possible outcome.

Autism – Some Psychoanalytic Perspectives

It is in such ways that psychoanalysis can indeed attempt to provide a different perspective from which to consider children described as autistic. On the one hand it offers a means of shifting the gaze from the pathologized to the pathologizer, whilst on the other hand it might be said to provide methods which are not only more acknowledging of individual experiences but which might also lead to a less obviously punitive treatment for the individual recipient.

Some work in psychoanalysis in the past has implied the possibility of an autistic phase of infant development but this theory has recently been eschewed by one of its original promoters. Frances Tustin (1994) concluded her life's work by declaring her developmentalized discourse upon autism to be erroneous but she continued to persist, however, in exploring the possibilities offered by the 'emotional aspects of autism' (1994a, p. 105).

Now, in marked contrast with the other, expert accounts of autism, but in similar vein to Tustin's work on the feelings experienced by children who are described as autistic, Donna Williams's words provide considerable evidence of her own emotional life. The words which Donna uses about herself, however – for example, 'afraid', 'gentle', 'magical' – are words which are not only her property, for they are words which any of us might use about ourselves. As such, they would not be sufficient to provide evidence of the earlier expert claims to Donna's 'abnormality', her 'emotional unresponsiveness' or her 'rigidity'. Indeed, Donna's words, exploring as they do her emotional and expressive life, seem to have little in common with the expert, medicalized and supposedly 'scientific' definitions of the nature of life which purport to define autism. Donna's words, I argue, appear far from abnormal, for her words can be prevalent amongst non-autistic people and would suggest that her feelings may well be similar to feelings experienced at one time or another by any of us.

It is not only the claims to Donna's emotional unresponsiveness made by the experts which I find remarkable but rather the degree of emotional sensitivity which she would claim for herself (she wrote of her 'emotional hypersensitivity'). In particular, Donna refers to 'terror', but especially her 'fear'; indeed, Donna's own account of what it is to be autistic (writing as she does in the joint position of being both a professional and a 'pathologized') seems filled with fear. Should we accept the validity of Donna's account, however, and then compare it with the expert accounts, we would have to declare that the words of the experts on p. 96 appear not to provide an accurate representation of Donna's experience. As both a professional and a 'pathologized', therefore, Donna might well claim authority over a mere professional who writes of her only as a 'pathologized'. In the same way, psychoanalytic readings, always by allowing for the possibility of an emotional sensitivity, could well make similar claims to provide a more scientific, more precise and valid account of autistic states than the more widely accepted view of the autistic person which tend to dictate current practices.

According to Donna, autistic experience includes very much the experience of being frightened. Autistic experience for her is being frightened of people, being frightened of closeness, being frightened of niceness, being frightened of losing control and being frightened of losing control over her feelings, 'autism is a protective reaction that develops to deal with the stress associated with a traumatic disruption ... autism being a reaction that is specific to trauma' (Tustin, 1994, p. 14). Donna's words, I suggest, are imbued with the 'common sense' notions of feeling which are again drawn from psychoanalysis by a psychology which would simultaneously deny their theoretical foundations, 'The paradoxical double operation which psychology compulsively repeats is to draw upon psychoanalytic notions, and to deny their truth' (Parker, 1997, p. 159).

Psychoanalytic readings of feelings and experience, I argue, can also be better equipped to accept the various abilities of the recipient (as opposed to their deficits) and also more able to resist simplistic interpretations and pathologizations. For example, Valerie Sinason's (1992) work with children regarded as having severe difficulties (whether they be related to learning, development or autistic states) always allows the possibility that the particular response of a child (or lack of) might be due, in one sense to the very intelligence of the child. In such work it is always possible that even the lack of response of a child might perhaps contain the enormity of their feelings/intelligence, rather than 'prove' their stupidity, indeed, 'Stupidity can be a defence against the trauma of knowing too much of a powerful kind' (Sinason, 1992, p. 7).

Psychoanalytic readings do not only concern the individual 'objects' of the pathologizer's gaze, however, for they also emphasize the presence of the analyst/professional, and allow us to reflect upon the nature of our own experience in the presence of a child. Such readings can, therefore, also allow us to see reasons as to why we might prefer to see a child's 'unresponsiveness' as a deficit rather than as positive evidence, for example, of their thinking and feeling, perhaps as a defence mechanism on our part. Not only do psychoanalytic readings allow for the capability of the child, therefore, they allow us to speculate that any of our responses might be due to our own particular 'deficit', 'Thinking the unthinkable means accepting a child's knowledge of terrible experiences ... it is easier to deny the emotional reality' (ibid., p. 209) and it is 'Far easier to see that M. is "seeking attention" than to feel the weight of their personal tragedy' (ibid., p. 232).

Donna's own admitted 'unresponsiveness', I argue, was scientific evidence, not of her lack of thinking/feeling, but of their very intensity. I had similarly speculated upon that possibility when I was with Peter and did so again with James. Let me provide brief examples in which I claim that I could see the evidence of feelings and thinking in both James and Peter (for different representations of these events see pp. 97–98).

Peter

I was watching Peter one day in the playground of his special school (see p. 97). There were several activities which I could have performed during the observation. Often, LEAs prefer information in the form of statistics (an approach which psychologists can seem to encourage), which can be produced by measurements such as counting or timing although sometimes it is the parents who ask me to perform intelligence testing. On this occasion I chose to watch Peter from perspectives which would be informed by psychoanalytic and interactionist approaches. I argue that this permitted me to see, unlooked for, something of beauty and intelligence for these seemed to be the characteristics of the way in which Peter played in the presence of the young girl. At first sight it might have appeared that Peter was playing alone but as I allowed myself a different mode, it seemed that I was allowing myself interpretations which could tolerate Peter's thinking and feeling in-relation-to this person who was touching his own orbit. Peter played around the tree, knowing the girl was just a few feet away and appearing to be very content in that knowing. As he looked at the girl a gesture of contact by him seemed to be agonisingly close, thus prompting my own thinking and feeling.

James

In contrast to this (I would say rather beautiful) scenario, I can place my experience of that earlier occasion on which James had been allocated the label of Asperger's Syndrome (p. 64). I did not challenge the decision for it was the province of another professional group. Shortly afterwards, however, at the end of that meeting, still angry at the (social) power of the scientific claims to certainty together with the reductionist view of James to which they would give rise, I went to see James in his class, which was basically a selfish act in which I sought some validation for my view of James, one in which we could share an unpathologized human nature:

> *I knelt by him.*
> *'Hello, James, it's really nice to see you.'*
> *He shivered. It was as if he was overflowing, as if perhaps the communication had been too perfect.*
> *'It's really nice to see you, Mr. Billington.'*

(Billington, 1997, p. 236)

The words I had spoken to James were somehow filled with more feeling than I had allowed myself to show previously and I argue that James sensed this (it could be argued that my actions were professionally inappropriate). Given that James's own feelings may conceivably be difficult for him to tolerate it seemed an act of remarkable bravery on his part that he did not raise his defences against those words and feelings of mine, and instead allowed them to touch him. I knew this to be so when his body shivered uncontrollably in response.

I am implying here, of course, a connection between words and feelings, one which might help to explain something of the interaction between James and myself. This is no mere professional hypothesis, however, for Donna Williams gives her own authoritative account of some possible connections in the light of her own experience, 'Words have no meaning when the thoughts have no feelings' (Williams, 1992, p. 146). She goes further, however, and suggests that, 'All thought begins with feeling' (p. 189). I argue that Donna, James and Peter all have human capacities for thinking and feeling which are poorly represented by the conventional models of psychopathology. Let me refer again to the particular example which I represented on p. 98, in 'Eyes II'.

One day James's classteacher brought him into the room to see me. He seemed 'out-of-sorts', restless and unhappy. James took the option of staying with me, however, possibly only because it was preferable to staying in his class but, whilst I talked and sought his interest, he played games at the desk. I continued to sense an irritability, however, and wondered whether it was merely my own. I could have closed the session, but I was interested in the way James kept putting his pencil sideways between his teeth and in the way that, by moving his head from side to side, he kept making sweeping gestures with the pencil point.

James was initially on another side of the desk, and despite obeying occasional requests from me to remove the pencil on safety grounds, somehow the pencil would always find its way back into his teeth and he would creep back closer to me. I was of course aware of the threat as the pencil point swept closer, but I was aware too, not only of my own feelings, but also of the possibly communicative possibilities of his actions. I chose to stop James when he came too close as I told him that he was likely to injure me. You will, as reader be able to decide upon your own interpretations of James's actions and also upon your own choice of action just as I did at the time.

I argue here that, had I relied solely on my professional training I would not have been able to acknowledge the complex nature of James's capacity for thinking, feeling and communication so clearly for training had not encouraged consideration of one's own anxieties as a legitimate resource. Such possibilities are rarely touched upon by psychological practices which can too often present individuals as objectified fragments of separated, dead objects.

Who is Knowing?

> Autistic people explain [that they are] so sensitive to sound when they are young that traffic noises are terrifying or painful and even the sound of their own blood in their ears makes an intolerable and ceaseless drumming ... young children with autism may also be hypersensitive to sights, smells, tastes and tactile sensations. Colours may be unbearably

vivid ... visual stimuli ... can cause distress; eye contact is frightening
and aversive. Touch may be experienced as unpleasant or even painful.
(Boucher, 1996, p. 83)

I met both Peter and his parents on several occasions during a period of nearly a
year before writing a draft report about him. Following a meeting at which I invited
Peter's parents to suggest alterations to the report, I wrote a further draft before
again inviting further comments from them. At this meeting, they questioned the
advisability of my remarks that, in school, Peter needed a 'stimulating environment'.
They criticized this because, in their experience, there was always a danger that
Peter could too easily become over-stimulated and become overwhelmed by the
number of stimuli with which he had to cope, and which can be a danger for many
children.

Now I had known this, but I had been concerned chiefly in this section of my
report to demand of the professionals with whom Peter was to work, an alertness of
mind which would enable their interactions with him to be of an intensely analytical
character and which would also be unerringly sympathetic to the nature of the
stimuli with which he was confronted. The stimulating environment had been inter-
preted as the availability of a quantity of stimulating objects whereas I had intended
to communicate the necessity for a quality of human response which would be characterized by that alertness to rich possibilities for action. This had been my attempt
to shift the gaze away from Peter's pathology to the professional skills from which
he might benefit. Thanks to the analytical powers of Peter's parents, the final report
eventually communicated this, perhaps, more succinctly, *'The emphasis should be
on, not Peter's failure (to communicate for example) but rather on adult abilities to
analyze and interpret his actions in order that Peter's learning needs can be met'*
(Author's report to the LEA under the 1993 Education Act).

A crucial point here, however, is not just the shift of gaze away from the
pathology and the concerns of the professionals, but also the recognizing of the
parents' ability to analyze, or know their own child. The educated, articulate
manner of the parents was such that it was possible for me to write, without challenge, that, *'In such cases parents become the experts in their child and they will
have accumulated much knowledge about Peter from which all professionals can
benefit'* (ibid.). These sentiments, however, may well have come under challenge had
I suggested it of parents who were not quite so articulate and whose social and
economic position was less powerful.

James and Peter were from broadly similar socio-economic backgrounds. James's
parents, however, were a little less assertive in dealing either with James or with
professionals. They also seemed relieved when the doctor allocated to James the
powerful words, 'Asperger's Syndrome'. Now, again, the power lies not in the words
themselves, the signifiers, but in the signified, which I argue here is the power over
the processes of pathologization. The allocation of a reductionist label, however,
seems to me to suggest a psychoanalytic dying in which as adults we are absolved
from the demand to engage actively with a child who is now confirmed as abnormal
in this way.

From the day of my first meeting with James in his school, I could well have predicted an eventual likely outcome/diagnosis, for his classteachers represented and pathologized him with words and phrases such as 'bizarre', 'he has repetitive behaviours', 'he doesn't initiate any social interaction', 'he won't give eye-contact'. It was indeed James's eyes which also held my attention. In my representations of those early meetings with him (pp. 97–98) I saw James often choosing to stare at objects for long periods and I wondered at the time just what he was thinking (or else avoiding) on such occasions. For example, did he stare in order to 'lose' himself in the sensory nature of the objects ('I learned to lose myself in anything I desired' – Donna Williams, 1992, p. 3)? Or did James stare, perhaps, to avoid looking at people (ibid., p. 122), 'looking into each other's eyes was the frightening feeling of losing oneself' and also my earlier representation, *Their eyes just once/Meeting, flashing /FEARING*' ('Eyes I', p. 97)?

Now some conventional expert accounts of 'autism' or 'Asperger's Syndrome' which relate to practice do not seem to concern themselves with complex possibilities, and would seem to imply that any behaviours might only be a physical phenomenon lacking in human quality, knowledge or feeling. James's use of his eyes, however, had always seemed to me to be purposeful and that he had decided to avert his eyes as a result of a knowledge which may well have been his acute awareness of my looking at him. Anne Alvarez describes a similar response in her work as a child psychotherapist as follows, 'It became increasingly obvious that he could go into these states almost at will for defensive purposes. ... He simply announced threateningly when he disliked the course a session was taking, "Mrs. Alvarez, I'm going to drift off", or "Mrs. Alvarez, I'm going to become Toby" ' (Alvarez, 1992, p. 39).

I remember two particular occasions in the early meetings with James when his eye contact neither appeared random nor vague. The second occasion was that which I related on p. 103 (when James 'shivered') but the first occasion had been on the first day I met him. James had just finished performing some 'ability' tests (at which he excelled incidentally, see pp. 63 and 68). As we left the room we walked into the hall and I saw a woman standing with her face close to the wall. Both James and the woman (I assumed her to be his mother) flashed a look at one another and quickly averted their eyes. James continued walking past and no other gesture of recognition was made by either of them. It seemed to me that the momentary meeting of their eyes had been so intense in some way that neither of them could bear it. This behaviour, however, seemed neither 'rigid' nor socially 'abnormal'; on the contrary, their behaviour seemed to have been an example of the sometimes unbearable nature of really *knowing* (see Sinason, 1992, p. 7).

Now Donna's representations would seem to indicate that the immediate aversion of her eyes was connected in some way to fear, whether it be fear of the other person, fear of losing oneself in the other person, or just fear of fear itself. I have little interest here as to the precise nature of either the fear or the knowing, whether of Donna, Peter or James (or James's mother). I do have an interest, however, in suggesting that these moments can possess – the individual can experience (or can defend themselves against) – intense, human qualities, of actually thinking and knowing. Should this be the case, it would be a travesty then to seek to rob Donna,

Peter or James of their knowing. Professionals can act, however, in ways which would deny their 'knowing', for example, by treating such children as 'abnormal', a categorization which would become an almost inevitable consequence of the allocation and subsequent circulation of a simple pathology.

It would be similarly misguided, however, and probably abusive, to lure any of these people away from the defences which they might have constructed against the immensity of such dangerous *knowing*, and upon which their psychological survival might well depend:

> The blackness I had to get to was the jump between 'my world' and 'the world', though I had never been able to make it in one piece. ... Too many well-meaning people would have tried mercilessly to drag me through the darkness unprepared, and killed my emotional self in the process. I may never have died physically, but psychically I had died many times in the effort. I had multiple fractures of the soul as a result.
>
> (Williams, 1992, p. 91)

Friends and Things

In Donna's autobiography she describes how certain people she met assumed another life inside her, becoming symbols and aspects of her personality which were necessary for her to survive in the world. Psychoanalysis provides a scientific basis upon which to theorize such phenomena:

> Melanie Klein ... discussed the manifold aims of different types of projective identification, for example, splitting off and getting rid of unwanted parts of the self into an object to dominate and control it and thus avoid any feelings of being separate; getting into an object to take over its capacities and make them its own; invading in order to damage or destroy the object. Thus the infant, or adult, who goes on using such mechanisms powerfully can avoid any awareness of any separateness, dependence, admiration, or its concomitant sense of loss, anger, envy, and so on.
>
> (Joseph, 1988, 168–169)

Now Donna seemed to people her world with her 'friends' in ways which resemble some of the types of projective identification above. I would argue that this could well have been the case with James. I selected the representations of James on pp. 97 and 98 ('Words', I and II) because of my speculations upon him and his friends. In response to my question, 'who are your friends?', James began to 'drift off' (see Alvarez, 1992). When I structured for James a possible response which allowed him to be positive and at the same time preserve his defences (and his friends?) intact, he chose to re-engage with me. Indeed, given the opportunity to initiate interaction, again in such a way as to leave his defences intact, James took the opportunity to ask me a question, 'how many friends have you?'

I speculate that this was no mere reframing of my question, which had been a question delivered without any great intelligence. Indeed, I speculate that James's initial responses to my questions about friends, together with his own question to me, contained a profound intelligence for which I was ill-prepared and to which I was initially ill-inclined. Valerie Sinason again points to the possibility that adults and professionals might have difficulty in acknowledging the thinking or knowing (of such pathologized children), a consequence of their own professionalized 'lack of' knowing – 'The disbelief ... in trying ... to consider the child's intelligence' (Sinason, 1992, p. 209). In contrast, one possible interpretation of James's question to me might even acknowledge it as evidence of his conceptual pre-occupation with one of life's great questions, for 'How many friends should you have?' (Aristotle, 1976, p. 307).

So James's question was sufficiently worthwhile for Aristotle to consider; unlike James, however, Aristotle had not been subjected to the same processes of pathologization. During the excellent work conducted by James's adult teaching assistant in school (which was, paradoxically, an economic resource delivered only after the allocation of the pathology), James sometimes revealed his own world of imaginary friends. James seemed to retreat to these friends at moments of danger, or perhaps even boredom, a state which might itself hold dangers for him. At what point does such mental activity become pathological, however, as opposed to necessary, pleasurable, or even creative and imaginative?

A year or so after this conversation with James, however, I visited him and his parents at home, and he introduced me to another aspect of his friends. I had spent an hour or so talking with his parents during the evening, amongst other things asking for their permission to include James and themselves in my research. I am sure that James followed every word that was spoken as he sat on the floor playing (a jigsaw) without a word for over half an hour (and this from a boy who was often noisy, active and disruptive in class and for whom, initially, 'AD/HD' – 'Attention Deficit/Hyperactivity Disorder' – was to have been diagnosed, p. 63).

Just as I was about to leave, James asked me, 'would you like to see my things?' He took me upstairs and on the landing at the top of the stairs stood an old chest of drawers. With a big effort, James opened one of the great drawers which was crammed full to overflowing with books. I realized that the 'things' to which James was proudly introducing me were his 'friends', and I was immediately aware of the importance and privilege of the moment. I hope that James could sense my own understanding of the value of the symbolic life which the books held for him, but the moment assumed a different quality when he asked of me, 'how many things have you?' (also see p. 98 for a different representation).

The question almost paralyzed me as I became even more aware of the importance of what was taking place and my intelligence, my own thinking/feeling had to stir in response to his. For James's 'friends' and/or 'things', I speculated, had a crucial role in his attempts to connect 'his world' with 'the world' outside of him. I speculated further that James's friends might not only be his means of controlling and mediating the world, however, but might offer a means of communicating. I refer again to Donna Williams's account:

For me the people I liked *were* their things. ... Communication via objects was safe. ... My world was full of [imaginary friends]. They were far more magical, reliable, predictable and real than other children, *and* they came with guarantees. It was a world of my own creation where I didn't need to control myself or the objects.

(Williams, 1992, pp. 5–8)

The importance of the moment which I had sensed as James pulled open the drawer could well have been my realization of the communicative nature of James's act. For James was not merely initiating social interaction, he was communicating with me. He was showing me his world and placing it in me. It would be vital, within this paradigm, to offer his world back to him undamaged. The truly communicative act on James's part, however, was that he was asking me to place part of my world back into him, for he asked, 'how many things have you?'

The cause of my paralysis was connected to my amazement once again at the bravery of James's act, for indeed, there could well have been dangers for him in lowering his defences so completely. This risk, however, could be a necessary leap for us all if we are ever to make Donna's 'jump' and connect ourselves to the world outside, to other 'friends' and 'things'.

In looking for a 'better way' of practising psychology, therefore, consider your own response to some other words, words which provide a very different representation of the kinds of experiences shared by Donna, Peter and James. For the following words claim to provide another 'clinical' definition of the mild form of 'autism' – the 'Asperger's Syndrome' which is supposed to be James, 'Severe impairment in reciprocal social interaction ... an all-absorbing, circumscribed interest in a subject ... a stereotyped way of trying to introduce and impose routines ... speech and language problems ... non-verbal communication problems ... motor clumsiness' (Gillberg and Gillberg, 1989; see also Billington 2000).

There was no evidence to suggest, as James pulled open the drawer, that the quality of his reciprocal social interaction was impaired. Neither could I see stereotyped behaviour, nor a problem with his communication, verbal or non-verbal. It is on the basis of such evidence that I am becoming inclined, therefore, to believe that a better, and perhaps even more scientific representation of human experience that is described as being 'Asperger's Syndrome' or 'autism' will be provided, not by a writer/psychologist/pathologizer – but by a 'pathologized' – the person pathologized. Furthermore, I might easily begin to take the position now that, hitherto, both the 'severe impairment' and the 'non-verbal communication problems', far from characterizing James, could well have been deficits in me, and perhaps hitherto in all the other professionals involved. However, in making such shifts, by averting the pathology away from James and on to the professional, we do not destroy the pathologizing tendency but merely alter the focus of its (social) gaze.

In mental space

If you sense distance, you're not mistaken; it's real.

(Williams, 1992, p. xviii)

> The more I kept to myself, or kept others at a distance, the clearer things
> became ... everything was reduced to colours, rhythms and sensations.
>
> (ibid., p. 60)

Donna's accounts of her experiences seem to describe a world, not of stereotypy, rigidity or emotional unresponsiveness, but a vivid world in which there is always movement, the activity of sensations and associated feeling and thinking, all taking place in a kind of vast mental cosmos. Some psychoanalytic accounts allow for these theoretical possibilities, 'The usual Kleinian formulations depend on a visual image of a space containing all kinds of objects. Into these objects in this space it is supposed that the patients project parts of their personality that they have split off' (Bion, 1970, p. 8).

Now Bion did not suggest that we can know such a mental space in its entirety as a 'thing-in-itself', but he does suggest that we can begin to represent it through our thoughts. Bion, however, sees possible dangerous implications for some in considering the processes of thinking and feeling, 'The mental realization of space is felt as an immensity so great ... that it cannot be represented at all' (ibid., p. 12). Bion's model for these processes, however, uses language which is far removed from reductionist definitions of autistic 'rigidity' or 'stereotypy' but explores instead exciting movements in space, constellations of sensations, feelings and thoughts which could be there for us all. This is not to say that particular patterns will not be repeated (NB: Bion's concept of 'beta-elements' on p. 112), but Bion's model of human learning and experience does invoke a conceptual universe in which the constituent parts are inexorably linked in ways which prohibit the usual simplistic fragmentations into individualized, static and pathologized atoms.

It is not within the scope of this book to provide a detailed account of Bion's work. Neither is it possible to explore here fully the potential of his speculations upon the nature of learning; for example, in finding alternative ways for working with children such as James and Peter. Nevertheless, it is incumbent upon me to keep close to the question of 'is there a better way of practising either education or psychology with children in which we might avoid either pathologizing or excluding them?'

Learning

The whole of Bion's 'model' for the ways in which learning can, or else may not take place depends on a very different conception of a science of learning. For Bion unashamedly bases his theory on a something, 'alpha-function', which he accepts does not exist in the usual sense:

> Alpha-function operates on the sense impressions, whatever they are, and the emotions, whatever they are, of which the patient [*sic*] is aware. In so far as the alpha-function is successful alpha elements are produced and these elements are suited to storage and the requirements of dream thoughts. If alpha-function is disturbed, and therefore inoperative, the sense impressions of which the patient

is aware and the emotions which he [*sic*] is experiencing remain unchanged. I shall call them beta-elements. In contrast with the alpha-elements the beta-elements are not felt to be phenomena, but things in themselves. Beta-elements are not amenable to use in dream thoughts but are suited for use in projective identification. … Beta-elements are stored but differ from alpha-elements in that they are not so much memories as undigested facts, whereas the alpha-elements have been digested by alpha-function and thus made available for thought.

(Bion, 1962, pp. 6–7)

Bion's 'model' for thinking, learning and *not* learning, is intrinsically interactive, a model for conceiving of thinking which is dependent upon the interaction between our sensory nature and our worlds, both within and without. Now Donna attested to the central role played by the sensations which she experienced (as have other 'autistic' autobiographers, for example, Grandin, in Grandin and Scariano, 1986), 'Autistic people explain [that they are] so sensitive to sound when they are young … young children with autism may also be hypersensitive to sights, smells, tastes and tactile sensations' (Boucher, 1996, pp. 82–83).

Far from being unresponsive to their environment, therefore, it would appear there is a another school of thought which would indicate that people described as 'autistic' might be hypersensitive to incoming stimuli. Now of course, it was Freud who pointed out that, 'Protection against stimuli is an almost more important function for the living organism than reception of stimuli' (Freud [1920], 1984, p. 299).

Peter's parents, of course, had really seemed to 'know' that stimuli could be stressful for him (see p. 105) just as Donna Williams articulated the link between her own incoming stimuli and the emotional consequences for her, 'The perceptual problems of deafness, dumbness and blindness … are caused by shutdown caused by extreme stress, brought on by the inability to cope with incoming information – often to do with emotions' (Williams, 1992, p. 181).

The general psychoanalytic concepts of projection and introjection provide a theoretical model for this movement and interaction, between an individual's sensations and their environmental context. Hinshelwood (1994) articulates the sensory nature of this process, and of its implications for our identity thus, 'The complex to-and-fro motion of the object in and out of the body; the very explicit experience of concrete internal objects … a clear link between bodily instincts and active relationships with objects' (p. 23) and 'Identity is bound up with the introjection of objects' (p. 58).

Now the 'incoming information' received by Donna, James and Peter, for example (but which, I argue, is received by all of us too) consists of the objects of the social world which we share. In this way any of our individual characteristics, should they be separated or fragmented from the individual whole, cannot be considered necessarily to be either our sole responsibility or indeed unique. Individual human experience, within Bion's theorization, can be characterized by the similarities which exist between us as we will all have access to broadly similar social and cultural 'objects' and 'stimuli'. In this way, it can be the individual characteristics of the social world which become crucial variables should we ever come to judge or assess the individual human being, '[Through] introjection and projection ... an inner world is built up which is partly a reflection of the external one' (Klein [1959], 1988, p. 250).

Hinshelwood's critique of the similarities between a Kleinian projective identification and a Marxian alienation implies that in both concepts, the individual will come to assume the characteristics of the society into which they are immersed. Should we accept a view that the emerging Western society of the last two or three hundred years is a pathological society, therefore, it is hardly surprising that individuals within that society too might become pathological, 'We see an increasing number of borderline personalities who are fragmented and exhibit primitive defence mechanisms, especially projective identification' (Hinshelwood, 1985, p. 250).

Bion sees the process of projective identification as the origins of thinking itself, a primitive means of dealing with the incoming (cultural) stimuli, 'The activity we know as "thinking" was in origin a procedure for unburdening the psyche of accretions of stimuli and the mechanism is that which has been described by Melanie Klein as "projective identification" ' (Bion, 1962, p. 31).

Bion's 'model' of mind suggests that thinking can be the activity of dealing with, or restricting the effects of incoming stimuli. He speculates upon the concept of 'alpha-function' which he sees as the way in which incoming stimuli are processed into 'alpha-elements' which in turn, he argues, then become available for further thought and phantasy.

Bion's model for thinking suggests that real thinking, intelligence and learning occur whenever we are able to tolerate the sensations which accompany the incoming stimuli. He suggests that for learning to take place we must be able to tolerate the frustration (feeling) which results from working with the living material, 'If the learner is intolerant of the essential frustration of learning he indulges in phantasies of omniscience and a belief in a state where things are known. [If the learner is intolerant of the essential frustration of learning] knowing something [will] consist in "having" some "piece" of knowledge and *not* in what I have called K' (ibid., p. 65).

Bion also suggests, however, that we will all experience occasions on which we will not be able to tolerate these incoming stimuli as all stimuli necessitate a 'feeling' response. It is on such occasions that alpha-function will not be able to transform the sensations into the alpha-elements which are necessary for future thinking and learning. Should alpha-function be inoperable we will, according to Bion's theory, instead engage in a process of primitive thought in which stimuli are transformed into 'beta-elements' – Bion refers to beta-elements as 'undigested facts'. As such, beta-elements allow no capacity for future learning as stimuli from without are experienced as objects within, deadened objects which have had their feeling/ thoughts removed, 'In practice it means that the patient feels surrounded not so much by real objects, things-in-themselves, but, by bizarre objects that are real only in that they are the residue of thoughts and conceptions that have been stripped of their meaning and ejected' (ibid., p. 99).

To Bion, knowing is not a singular, temporal fragment of a something which can be captured, disconnected and fossilized. Bion's argument is that knowing ('K') is a process, that he calls a 'function'. This process of knowing is dialectical, and the process of knowing, 'K', consists of opposing 'factors', which he names as love ('L') and hate ('H'), which are themselves activity. Bion's hypothetical model for knowing, therefore, is a relationship, a moving, dialectical process in which 'L', 'H' and 'K' exist and operate only in so far as they are *in-relation-to* one another. Should the individual constituents be separated from one another, the result will be to remove the living force from each element. In the construction of the illusion of knowledge, therefore, I argue that Bion's 'model' suggests that, ultimately, the living world is unknowable.

Now I am not here restricting the application of this model of learning to a particular category. Bion's model for learning and knowing provides a conceptual, scientific and analytic position from which to base professional work; a position from which we could seek to avoid the illusion of the category. For I argue that Bion's model of thinking and learning is a model which can tolerate (but rather depends upon) relationships which occur in space/movement/time.

A truly dialectical, active model of learning and knowing is very different from the model of thinking and learning which I suggest predominates in the English education system and which also predominates in both the training and the practices of its professionals. I suggest that, too often, many of the practices of both education and child psychology in England are based upon thinking which is stripped of its vitality and organized in beta-elements, and are thus characterized by the accretion of 'pieces' of dead knowledge. These 'pieces' of knowledge merely substitute for a more active thinking and learning which, by comparison, are characterized by move- ment and relations-to, which are able to tolerate stimuli and which, crucially, are able to tolerate the uncertainty of *not knowing*. This may not be surprising should we accept Bion's view that, ' "Thinking" in the sense of engaging in that activity which is concerned with the use of thoughts, is embryonic even in the adult and has yet to be fully developed in the race' (ibid., p. 85).

In the cases of Donna, Peter and James there have been common professional judgements made about the ways in which they think and learn. Often, of course, these acts have not been committed directly, but have occurred as part of a process in which certain individuals are selected for immersion into discourses of deficit such as 'stereotypy' and 'rigidity'. The outcomes for those chosen in this process will usually include a restriction upon their social and economic opportunities and the denial of their thinking, their knowing and their abilities to learn.

No such judgement, however, has been possible regarding the nature of the professional thinking upon which these pathologizations have relied, for the focus has been firmly fixed on those who are the recipients of the pathology. Indeed, I argue that Donna, Peter and James, rather than receiving help from the professionals (which is an implicit discourse more commonly associated with us), have often been under attack from us (possibly Bion's 'H').

Now Donna Williams suggested some ways in which professionals, and indeed any person, could conduct social interactions (i.e. providing her with incoming stimuli and receiving her communications) which would have been more acceptable to her. She writes directly about the occasions on which she could tolerate the incoming stimuli of social relationships:

What I liked [about teacher] ... was that there were no wrong answers.
(Williams, 1992, p. 42)

My father had all the right responses; he simply sat within my presence, letting me show him how I felt in the only way I could – via objects.

(ibid., p. 67)

I had reached out to Mary [psychiatrist] as somebody I could 'trust' in the world. She had accepted me as more than a patient; she had accepted me personally.

(ibid., p. 108)

Bryn [friend] would simply come and exist in my company.

(ibid., p. 121)

I am reminded again here of my visit to Peter's class (p. 97). In a professional world of dead 'strategies', 'targets' and manic 'doing', it can be difficult to sustain the validity of a physical inactivity, which is often now to resist the demand for quantity. It may be, however, that to encourage learning, it would be better for us to experience, not ever increasing stimuli in whatever form, but alternatively living moments and *relations-to* in which we can come to tolerate our own frustration, the feelings which can activate the process and activity of our (social) thinking and learning.

I argue, however, that the social processes to which Donna, Peter and James have been subjected have too often not provided such space for their learning but have instead surrounded them with dead artefacts. They have been under attack from professionals who have themselves been employed to introject dead or alienated cultural objects or discourses from the rest of society in order to insert them, as individual 'pieces' of knowledge, beta-elements, stripped of their vitality and meaning, into other human targets.

This representation is of a process of pathologization in which James, Peter and Donna have all become receptacles for our own social death together with a cultural and psychological alienation, 'It is a schizoid society in which we live. This is alienation' (Donna Williams, 1992, p. 123). The individual artefacts or signifiers projected into Donna, James and Peter may indeed be dead, mere words stripped of their vitality and meaning. The processes of pathologization, however, are the signified which move along the metonymic axis, and they are not dead.

I argue that the processes of pathologization, separation and exclusion incorporate elements which include sympathy and human concern and the provision of 'special' help, 'L', together with representations of hate and the exclusion of particular categories, 'H', in a process of 'minus K'. Indeed, the whole search for a static, knowable, knowledge (which has become the search for categories) may well be represented by Bion's concept of the function of 'minus K' in which, 'elements are stripped of their meaning and only the worthless residue is retained' (Bion, 1962, p. 98). I suggest that in such social relations, of 'minus K', we might see the processes of alienation, social processes in which, through the construction and pursuit of knowledge, we desperately seek to avoid the awfulness of knowing.

Endpiece

It is important for me to reiterate at this point that it has not been my intention in this section to provide a complete, hermetically sealed conceptual framework based on psychoanalysis, either for working with children or for working with children whose behaviours have been pathologized in particular ways. Bion would concur:

> The mental domain cannot be contained within the framework of psychoanalytic theory. ... It would be a valid observation to say that psycho-analysis cannot 'contain' the mental domain because it is not a 'container' but a 'probe'.
>
> (Bion, 1970, p. 73)

Indeed, processes similar to such psychoanalytic concepts as 'projective identification' and 'counter-transference', for example, have long been known in different forms to many others inside Western culture, and known to those who have lived outside, and indeed before, psychoanalysis, for example, in philosophy: 'He [*sic*] who imagines that which he loves to be affected by pleasure or pain will also be affected by pleasure or pain', (Spinoza, 1989, Prop. XXI, p. 99) and 'In every passion of which the mind of man [*sic*] is susceptible, the emotions of the bystander always correspond to what, by bringing home to himself, he imagines should be the sentiments of the sufferer', (Smith [1759], 1982, p. 10).

The chapter has, rather, been an exercise in speculation in which I have sought to provide a critique for my own professional practices as a child psychologist working within the education system. It has constituted activity in which I have sought to avoid the destructive and stigmatizing (Levett, 1995) acts of pathologization by speculating upon ways of representing thinking and learning which focus upon *relations-to* rather than on individual categories or characteristics.

These chapters have constituted further activity in which I have searched for more critical psychological practices and are intended to contribute to a larger social debate which begs consideration of the moral and ethical basis for professionals who work with children in the name of education or psychology.

Suggestions for Further Reading

Donna Williams continues to write of her experiences and any of her books will provide useful points from which to reflect upon professional practices in relation to autism.

Wilfred Bion's books are not necessarily easy for the uninitiated but for those already at ease with post-Kleinian psychoanalytic thinking (or else for those who enjoy a challenge) they allow fascinating connections to be made between feelings, thinking, learning and language (NB: in particular, *Learning From Experience*).

9 Conclusion
Discourse on Science

Demonstrable truths, and every kind of scientific knowledge (because this involves reasoning) depend on first principles. It follows that the first principles of scientific truths cannot be grasped by science or art or by prudence ... the state of mind that apprehends first principles is intuition.

(Aristotle, 1976, p. 210)

This book may contain some truths but its primary claim is that it is text. The words, of course, are not *my* words for I don't own them, as they are symbolic forms inherited from a collective social and cultural lexicon. I have merely been re-arranging the words into particular shapes and constellations of sound and meaning, perhaps in the way of a sculptor or a composer, or indeed as a writer. Some of the analytical methods chosen therefore, in particular discourse analysis and psycho-analysis, do not accept that words necessarily 'speak for themselves' and I reiterate that there are 'things beyond language'. In making occasional recourse to literature too I have thus sought representations of experience which beg consideration of the relationship between words and the (human) living which is beyond them.

Any authorial position may be less than precise, therefore, and I have thus sought to avoid making claims to accurate truths of others, which, however, can characterize the demands of my work with individual children and their parents as a psychologist employed in the education system. Indeed, a principle throughout has been the need to challenge some of the assumptions underpinning the social activities generated, circulated and subsequently protected by professional practices which are necessarily subject to employers' demands. I have thus searched for less oppressive ways of seeing children not least because, 'The issue is to bring to light, acknowledge, the investment and hidden subjectivity that lie beneath the claims to disinterested, true knowledge' (Burman, 1994, p. 188). The search has not been necessarily for knowledge, therefore, but rather the ways in which knowledge is claimed and becomes subject to powers of ownership.

Neither has the search been merely for 'method'. Rather, I have been writing as a means of re-engaging with my own 'knowing' or intuition. In contrast, the conditions in which many of us work with children hinder such 'knowing' by distracting us and indeed burying us with innumerable pieces of information produced in the name of a science in which, 'The context stripping that takes place as part of a positivist endeavour makes the knowledge generated often unusable' (Figg and Richards, 1999). In such processes, the separating, losing and excluding of the book's title are not merely experienced by others, however, for they will be known to us too and endured through our own professional practices.

The kinds of scientific 'knowing' which I have utilized are informed by the 'intuition' and 'intelligence' which, to Aristotle, were interchangeable (see editor's footnote in Aristotle, 1976, p. 211). Aristotle's understanding of 'intelligence', imbued as it was with the sense both of 'activity' and of 'intuition', seems to represent a kind of 'knowing' which I have also detected in a range of other, seemingly diverse disciplines and theories, for example, not only psychoanalysis (Bion) but also literature (Berger) and even mathematics too (see Hofstadter, 1980 in Billington, 1997). Such authors have refuted any simplistic reduction to 'knowledge', for their representations are of a moving world, invested with the qualities and activities of human lives, which are never still. This kind of 'knowing', I argue after Aristotle, is both intelligence and intuition, which is, 'The immediate perception of truth' (Tredennick, in Aristotle, 1976, p. 211).

Just as 'knowing' and 'truth' cannot be totally contained by their representation in the form of words, however, neither can they be contained by a model of human science which is based on a simple 'medical materialism' (see James [1902], 1982). For such a model lacks the capacity to hold the dialectical co-existence, interaction and inter-dependency of the infinite complexity of human conditions, as well as its simultaneous, crushing simplicity. Some approaches to human science do not have the capacity to tolerate the possibility of a human world beyond themselves and there is a vigorous contemporary cultural thrust to restrict the truths of human experience to stories of the biological, clinical and neurological. Whilst there can be many benefits in the manufacture of such specialisms by professionals, there is a danger in keeping invisible the alliance between economic and political movements on the one hand and on the other hand those merely technological developments which are endeavouring to lay claim to the very truths of human experience and causality.

Now it has not been my intention to undermine either the existence of knowledge or the capacities of individuals, professionals or otherwise to be in a state of knowing something. I have, rather, attempted to adopt more questioning scientific positions which can remain intelligent to the power of particular economic and political processes. I have also tried to adopt positions in this book which keep alive the philosophical, ethical and moral stories of human experience lest they too be overwhelmed by a kind of epistemological totalitarianism.

Such positions are too easily claimed by child professionals and in the processes children are often denied the possibility of their own 'knowing', thus reinforcing the acts of separating and fragmenting which are a focus for this book. As part of the resistance I have also advocated the need for child professionals to be aware of their power as story-tellers and their need also to become historians who possess some understanding of social, economic and political processes in order that they might 'ward off the psychologization of political problems' (Burman, 1997, p. 146).

Adult discourses about children have become infused with 'difficulties' which emanate from a supposed scientific rigour. However, I have tried to make contact again with a *spirit* of scientific inquiry which has too often been eschewed since a nineteenth-century schism, 'We can find by 1867 ... the word 'science' ... as expressing physical and experimental science, to the exclusion of the theological and metaphysical' (Williams, 1976, p. 278). In searching for my own 'knowing', therefore, I have been searching for 'science'. In the process I have deployed various available resources in order to resist the non-science of many current, preferred practices, searching instead for a genuinely interactive model which can tolerate the complexity of human relations, 'What is required is ... a science that is not restricted by its genesis in knowledge and sensuous background. It must have a mathematics of at-one-ment, not identification. There can be no geometry of 'similar', 'identical', 'equal', only of analogy' (Bion, 1970, p. 89).

It has also been another principle, however, that in order to reflect upon the nature of my own activities, I need to consider outcomes. I will, therefore, make one or two final, brief representations, of Gary, Mary, James and Peter. I have not met Gary since the writing of Chapter 2 (which was several years ago now) and I know nothing of what may have happened to him. To contact him now would seem cynical but this situation seems to highlight the extent of the disciplinary commitment (by education or psychology) and also my own personal lack of commitment to him. I meet up to one hundred children every year and I see few of them beyond the immediate assessment period. One of the outcomes in Gary's case, therefore, is that neither child psychology nor education will be required to adjudicate in any further exclusions, as he will now have long since left school. In view of the book title, however, it should be noted that Gary was not removed from his school prior to his natural finishing date, which had initially seemed likely.

I met with Mary occasionally over a period of three years, primarily in order to resist any further attempts to remove her from school but to the teachers' great credit, they made huge efforts to accommodate her 'difference'. At the last meeting with her I asked whether she would need to see me again. She was sufficiently kind not to say 'no' too bluntly, but increasingly, she seemed irritated by my presence and she did not respond to my offer of further involvement. I was later contacted by a senior manager at the school, at one point to seek my advice regarding Mary's request to have a 'work experience' placement in an early years centre, and again during the following year in order to inform me that, whilst Mary had left home she had stayed at school to the very end of Year 11. She had even taken some examinations. Mary was viewed by many at the school to have been one of their great successes and the various professionals involved were able to share their acknowledgement of this.

Peter has played a relatively minor part inside this book but this is not a reflection of my involvement over the years with his parents. Peter's parents (and Peter too I believe) became increasingly frustrated by the disinclination of professionals either to meet him with their own intelligence or else to tolerate his. Some years on now, and despite his parents' misgivings, following a period in a residential school, Peter is back living in the home as all involved struggle to find a suitable educational placement.

For James, the process of 'Statementing' meant the allocation of a very poorly paid welfare assistant ('May') in order to act as his 'minder' in primary school. The provision of May as a simple economic resource, however, was sufficient to keep James in the school. This account, however, fails to do justice to his parents' best efforts, the school's 'good-enough' commitment to him and not least May's own particular awesome powers of advocacy and protection. The particular relationship which grew between James and May was characterized by a vigorous sharing of their intelligences. The quality of their relationship, however, would be impossible to assess within the bounds of a mere mechanistic science and this highlights a possible direction of future work for, 'A science of relationships has yet to be established' (Bion, 1970, p. 53).

I argue, therefore, that as well as becoming historians, child professionals would benefit from education and training which puts a much greater emphasis on those questions of ethics, morality, history and philosophy from which developmental psychology, for example, has too often become separated. Whilst some positivist scientists and clinicians grow ever more bullish in their claims, for example, 'I believe that in the twenty first century the ancient philosophical mind-body problem will be solved – not by philosophers but by scientists' (Dawkins, 1999), I am reminded again that, 'Old age has the last word; the purely naturalistic look at life, however enthusiastically it may begin, is sure to end in sadness. This sadness lies at the heart of every merely positivistic, agnostic or naturalistic scheme of philosophy' (James [1902], 1982, p. 140). I suggest, therefore (after Bion), that we need to develop a 'science of relationships' in order to resist the separating and excluding which currently characterize our practices with children – practices which are too often subservient to political discourses of (dis)ability, gender, race and social class.

It is necessary to keep alive such ways of thinking for the industrialization of human differences continues unabated. The specialized forms of work made possible by the division of labour have developed even more specialized forms and through the continuing expansion of market capacity we are fast reaching a point at which, amazingly, new technologies are now offering the prospect of the eradication of all differences. Such a prospect demands that we recognize, not merely the political and economic investments at stake in such an enterprise, but the importance of asking difficult questions. For what differences do we celebrate (Bird, 1999)? What differences do we tolerate? What differences do we abhor, and at what point can the processes of a punitive pathologization inherent within the new technological developments be brought to a halt? (see Billington, 1999).

We might place ourselves against such ideas, or rather practices, for whilst the efforts of professionals and their developing technologies have helped many of us to enjoy healthier, longer lives, at what point will a regulatory authority in the future be involved in creating laws regarding potential progeny? What will be the criteria? White, black? Male, female? Parental background? Parental biological history? What level of predicted ability/disability will be acceptable? It is in such questions that we see the discourses and dilemmas of care and control to which children are subject.

I will conclude with one final narrative. May, the 'mere' welfare assistant who committed herself to James so expertly (and who is paid but a small fraction either of a teacher's wage or indeed that of a psychologist) was allocated to him by the

LEA purely by chance. It was, then, coincidence that at the time, May had her own 16-year-old son, John, who had been diagnosed 'autistic'. Several years ago now, May asked if I could take responsibility for his 'case' prior to his entry into a new phase of education. One warm, summer's morning, during the first home visit, John made polite conversation with me for quite a long time, offered me a cup of tea and then left the room. May then began to tell me something of John's earlier years, of her determined fight to keep him in a mainstream high school but, prior to that, of his screaming fits when he first started at primary school. May then showed me some of John's attempts at written representation of those first classroom experiences.

Briefly, before considering John's words, let me re-present the 'three (capitalized) lies' relating to human ability, quality and value which owe much to Adam Smith's original analyses of the emerging economic conditions over two centuries ago:

- children with particular abilities are necessarily worth more than children without such abilities;
- these abilities can be categorized and measured;
- these abilities are static and necessarily (self-)contained within an individual child.

For with what certainty can we declare children such as Gary, Mary, Peter, James and John to be 'worth less than ... ' and with what certainty can we claim that we have the skills to measure accurately their human talents, qualities and potentials? I have argued that in the performance of many activities child professionals often contribute to the harmful consequences of separating and excluding. Given that, should not we instead develop scientific practices which can resist these processes and which can also hold as central the human experience and intelligence of which John himself was aware at the age of 9? The following words were written at the time by him to describe his primary school classroom:

> *'The whole place was wobbly and rockly* [sic] *with noise and everything was moving, there was big smells and all the things were different, it was full of dark noise and light noise and echoes and growly voices.'*

I argue that it is possible to declare with more certainty that the application of a merely positivist science towards human abilities tells us only a little about John, Gary, Mary, Peter or James for it tells us only a little about their human experiences, their intelligences and qualities. It is by keeping alive stories of human experience which can recognize such qualities that further resistances to the pathologizing tendency will be found. It is by preserving our abilities to conceive of such stories that we might continue to challenge some of the prevailing assumptions in our work with children and develop new emancipatory resistances to the stigmatizing and exclusionary outcomes of many current practices.

Now whilst such narrative forms might provide a focus for collective resistances against alienating forms of professional practice, the daily dilemmas posed by social circumstances which are inherently individualizing and fragmenting will continue to demand decisions in the shape of advice which we might give and strategies from which we should choose at the individual level. Paradoxically, however, we might connect with children and their learning by keeping alive the vitality of our own experience of learning, and by acknowledging our own lives in our work with them for:

> Education is a difficult and complicated affair only as long as we wish to educate our children, or anyone at all, without educating ourselves. But if we understand that we can only educate others through ourselves, then the question of education lapses, and we are left only with the question of living: how ought one to live oneself?
>
> (Tolstoy, in Christian, 1978, p. 532)

The challenge for us now is to develop, both for children and professionals, approaches to education which help to preserve rather than deny the real of our experience, the question of living.

Notes

2 Gary – A Formal Assessment

1 Division of labour. This is a term to be found in the works of Adam Smith, the eighteenth-century philosopher, economist and 'Historian', and is still used widely. It has specific associations with the separation of employments, trades and skills into specialist activities. It will be considered at greater length in Chapter 6.
2 Regulation and resistance. These are co-existing possibilities in public actions which are linked, according to Michel Foucault, the French philosopher/psychologist/historian. Their inter-dependency allows for the complexity of power relations in governmental arenas without ever denying the potential for individual agency. As such, they relate to much of the material in the book.
3 Observation. This is a standard tool in psychological assessment. However, Foucault offers surveillance as a general governmental activity which can be found across many sites of professional endeavour (e.g. the prison, the hospital, the school).
4 Some LEAs set criteria against which particular needs can be assessed. In my employing LEA, psychologists are asked to provide psychometric information relating to a child's abilities (i.e. through tests of 'intelligence') and attainments (i.e. scores for reading, spelling and number).

3 Pathologizing Children: Power and Regulation

1 The Warnock Report (DES, 1978) surmised that about 18 per cent of all children would experience some form of special educational needs during their school career.
2 'Technologies of government' is a term employed by Rose and Miller (1992) which can be applied to those practices which professionals devise in order to perform governmental activities more effectively. For example, the design of more sophisticated tests, whilst assisting the professional, may have few benefits for the child recipient and may well share similar regulatory possibilities with older, less refined technologies.

6 Memory, History and the Division of Labour

1 Estimates: estimation formed part of the quantitative methodology used in previous research (see Billington, 1993).
2 Freud and Marx were two late-nineteenth-century figures whose ideas had a profound influence in twentieth-century culture. Freud, of course, emphasized the intra-psychic aspects of our lives (although not exclusively) whilst Marx emphasized the inherently social nature of human existence (although, again, not exclusively).
3 See Walkerdine, 1988, for further exploration of this point.

7 Alienation or Pathology?

1 Psychopathologist: currently, this can refer to almost anyone but specific control over categories rests still mainly with medical practitioners, but sometimes psychologists and educationalists too.

2   Marx's *Economic and Philosophical Manuscripts* and *Grundrisse* were amongst many of his works which, following translation, only entered Western culture more generally after the Second World War.

3   Alienation: not least of the problems with the word are its various translations from various related words in German (see Williams, 1976).

4   Marx makes a further link to the processes of surplus value (see Smith [1776], 1970 and Marx [1857–8], 1977).

5   Some research is now also being conducted on the unborn child's relations and experiences inside the womb e.g. Piontelli, 1992.

References

Alvarez, A. (1992) *Live Company*, London: Tavistock/Routledge.

American Psychiatric Association (1994) *Diagnostic and Statistical Manual*, 4th edition.

Aristotle (1976) *Ethics*, Tredennick, H. (ed.), London: Penguin Classics.

Arthur, C. (1982) 'Objectification and alienation in Marx and Hegel', in *Radical Philosophy*, 30, Spring, 14–24.

Bakhtin, M. (1984) *Problems of Dostoevsky's Poetics*, Emerson, C. (ed.), University of Manchester Press.

Barton, L. (ed.) (1989) *Disability and Dependency*, Sussex: Falmer Press.

Benjamin, W. (1992) *Illuminations*, Arendt, H. (ed. and trans.), London: Fontana Press.

Berger, J. (1989) *Into Europa*, London: Granta Books.

—— (1990) *Lilac and Flag*, London: Granta Books.

—— (1992) *Pig Earth*, London: Chatto and Windus.

Billig, M., Condor, S., Edwards, D., Gane, M., Middleton, D. and Radley, A. (1988) *Ideological Dilemmas: A Social Psychology of Everyday Thinking*, London: Sage.

Billington, T. (1993) 'Sex differences in student estimations of student–teacher interaction', in *Research in Education*, November, 50, 17–26.

—— (1995) 'Acknowledging interpretation in everyday practice: a discourse analytic approach', in *Educational Psychology in Practice*, 11 (3), 36–45.

—— (1996) 'Pathologizing children: psychology in education and acts of government', in Burman, E. et al., *Psychology, Discourse Practice: Regulation and Resistance*, London: Taylor and Francis.

—— (1997) 'Separating, losing and excluding children: readings in a critical psychology', Ph.D. thesis, Department of Psychology and Speech Pathology, Manchester Metropolitan University.

—— (1999) 'Feminist questions and educational psychology', in *Educational and Child Psychology*, 16 (2), 27–34.

—— (2000) 'Words, pathologies and children', in Moore, M. (ed.), *Insider Perspectives on Inclusion: Raising Voices, Raising Issues*, Sheffield: Philip Armstrong Press.

—— (2000a) 'Working with parents: autism: discourses in experience, expertise and learning', in *Educational Psychology in Practice*, 16 (1), 59–68.

Bion, W. (1970) *Attention and Interpretation*, London: Karnac Books.

—— (1962) *Learning from Experience*, London: Karnac Books.

Bird, L. (1999) 'Feminist questions about children's competence', *Educational and Child Psychology*, 16 (2), 17–26.

Boucher, J. (1996) 'The inner life of children with autistic difficulties', in Varma, V. (ed.), *The Inner Life of Children with Special Needs*, London: Whurr Publishers.

Burman, E. (1994) *Deconstructing Developmental Psychology*, London: Routledge.

—— (1997) 'Telling stories: psychologists, children and the production of "false memories"', *Theory and Psychology*, 7 (3), 291–309.

—— (1997a) 'Developmental psychology and its discontents', in Fox, D. and Prilleltensky, I. (eds), *Critical Psychology: an Introduction*, London: Sage.

Burman, E. and Parker, I. (eds) (1993) *Discourse Analytic Research: Repertoires and Readings of Texts in Action*, London: Routledge.

Burman, E., Alldred, P., Bewley, C., Goldberg, B., Heenan, C., Marks, D., Marshall, J., Taylor, K., Ullah, R., Warner, S. (1996) *Challenging Women: Psychology's Exclusions, Feminist Possibilities*, Buckingham: Open University Press.

Burman, E,. Aitken, G., Alldred, P., Allwood, R., Billington, T., Goldberg, B., Gordo Lopez, A., Heenan, C., Marks, D., Warner, S. (1996a) *Psychology, Discourse Practice*, London: Taylor and Francis.

Christian, R.F. (ed. and transl.) (1978) *Tolstoy's Letters*, London: Athlone.

Clough, P. and Barton, L. (1995) *Making Difficulties*, London: Paul Chapman.

Cooter, R. (ed.) (1992) *In the Name of the Child*, London: Routledge.

Dawkins, R., in Griffiths, S. (ed.) (1999) *Predictions*, Oxford: Oxford University Press.

Department for Education and Science (1978) *Warnock Report*, HMSO.

—— (1981) *Education Act*, HMSO.

Department for Education and Employment (1993) *Education Act*, HMSO.

—— (1994) *The Code of Practice*, HMSO.

Derrida, J. (1975) 'The purveyor of truth', in *Yale French Studies*, 52, 31–113.

Dickens, C. [1860–61] (1993) *Great Expectations*, Cardwell, M. (ed.), Oxford: Oxford's World Classics.

Duden, B. in Sachs, W. (ed.) (1992) *The Development Dictionary: A Guide to Knowledge as Power*, London: Zed Press.

Eliot, G. [1871–2] (1996) *Middlemarch*, Carroll, D. (ed.), London: Oxford University Press.

—— [1879] (1995) *The Impressions of Theophrastus Such*, Enright, D.J. (ed.), London: J.M. Dent.

Figg, J. and Richards, A. (1999) 'Feminism in psychology and professional contexts: professional and educational psychology practices', *Educational and Child Psychology*, 16 (2), 62–66.

Foucault, M. (1967) *Madness and Civilisation*, London: Routledge.

—— (1970) *The Order of Things*, London: Tavistock.

—— (1977) *Discipline and Punish: The Birth of the Prison*, London: Allen Lane.

—— (1979) 'On governmentality', in *Ideology and Consciousness*, 6, 5–21.

Freud, S. [1900] (1976) *The Interpretation of Dreams*, London: Pelican Books.

—— [1915–17] (1973) *Introductory Lectures in Psychoanalysis*, London: Penguin.

—— [1920] (1984) 'Beyond the pleasure principle', in *On Metapsychology*, London: Penguin.

Fromm, E. [1942] (1984) *The Fear of Freedom*, London: Ark.

Frosh, S. (1987) *The Politics of Psychoanalysis*, Basingstoke: Macmillan Education.

—— (1989) *Psychoanalysis and Psychology*, Basingstoke: Macmillan Education.

Genette, G. (1980) *Narrative Discourse*, translated by Jane E. Lewin, Oxford: Basil Blackwell.

Georgaca, E. (1995) 'Things beyond language? Lacan and Kristeva', presentation at the *Discourse Unit, Manchester Metropolitan University*, March 20th.

Gillberg, I.C. and Gillberg, C. (1989) 'Asperger's Syndrome: some epidemiological considerations', in *Journal of Child Psychology and Psychiatry*, 30, 631–638.

Grandin, T. and Scariano, M.M. (1986) *Emergence: Labeled Autistic*, Novato, CA: Arena Press.

Haug, F. (1992) 'The Hoechst Chemical Company and boredom with the economy', in *Beyond Female Masochism: Memory Work and Politics*, London: Verso.

Henriques, J., Hollway, W., Urwin, C., Venn, C. and Walkerdine, V. (1984) *Changing the Subject*, London: Methuen.

Hinshelwood, R.D. (1983) 'Projective identification and Marx's concept of man', in *International Review of Psycho-Analysis*, 10, 221–226.

—— (1985) 'Projective identification, alienation and society', in *Group Analysis*, 18/3, 241–254.

—— (1994) *Clinical Klein*, London: Free Association.

—— (1996) 'Convergences with psycho-analysis', in Parker, I. and Spears, R. (eds), *Psychology and Society*, London: Pluto Press.

Hobsbawm, E.J. (1962) *The Age of Revolution 1789–1848*, London: Sphere Books.

—— (1975) *The Age of Capital 1848–1875*, London: Abacus.

—— (1987) *The Age of Empire 1875–1914*, London: Abacus.

—— (1995) *The Age of Extremes*, London: Abacus.

Hofstadter, D. (1980) *Gödel, Escher, Bach: an Eternal Golden Braid*, London: Penguin Books.

Hollway, W. (1989) *Subjectivity and Method in Psychology*, London: Sage.

Jakobson, R. (1962) *Selected Writings*, The Hague: Mouton.

James, W. [1902] (1982) *The Varieties of Religious Experience*, London: Penguin Books.

References

Joseph, B., in Spillius, E.B. (ed.) (1988) *Melanie Klein Today*, vol. 1 *Mainly Theory*, London: Routledge.

Kierkegaard, S. (1989) *The Sickness Unto Death*, London: Penguin Classics.

Klein, M. (1988) *Envy and Gratitude and Other Works 1946–1963*, London: Virago.

—— [1932] (1989) *The Psychoanalysis of Children*, London: Virago.

Lacan, J. (1972) 'Seminar on the purloined letter', in *Yale French Studies*, translated Mehlman, J., 48, 38–72.

—— (1977) *Écrits*, London: Routledge.

Laplanche, J. and Pontalis, J.-B. (1988) *The Language of Psychoanalysis*, London: Karnac Books.

Levett, A. (1995) 'Stigmatic factors in sexual abuse and the violence of representation', in *Psychology in Society*, 20, 4–12.

Lukacs, G. [1937] (1962) *The Historical Novel*, translated Mitchell, H. and S., London: Merlin Press.

MacIntyre, A. (1981) *After Virtue: A Study in Moral Theory*, London: Duckworth.

Mandel, E.M. and Novack, G. (1970) *The Marxist Theory of Alienation*, London: Pathfinder Press.

Marcuse, H. (1966) *Eros and Civilization*, Boston: Beacon Press.

Marx, K. (1844) *The Economic and Philosophical Manuscripts* in McLellan, D. (ed.) (1977), *Karl Marx: Selected Writings*, Oxford: OUP.

—— (1857–8) *Grundrisse* in McLellan, D. (ed.) (1977), *Karl Marx: Selected Writings*, Oxford: OUP.

McLean, C. (1995) 'A conversation with Noam Chomsky', in Schooling and Education, *Dulwich Centre Newsletter*, nos 2 and 3, Adelaide.

Meszvaros, I. (1970) *Marx's Theory of Alienation*, London: Merlin Press.

Murray, L. (1998) *Collected Poems*, London: Carcanet Press.

Nagel, T. (1979) *Mortal Questions*, Cambridge: Cambridge University Press.

—— (1986) *The View From Nowhere*, Oxford: Oxford University Press.

Newman, F. and Holzman, L. (1993) *Lev Vygotsky: Revolutionary Scientist*, London: Routledge.

Ollmann, B. (1971) *Alienation: Marx's Concept of Man in Capitalist Society*, Cambridge: Cambridge University Press.

Pansini, G. (1997) 'The structure of internal space: conditions for change in a 6-year-old girl with severe developmental delay', in *Journal of Child Psychotherapy*, 23 (1), 25–50.

Parker, I. (1992) *Discourse Dynamics*, London: Routledge.

—— (1996) 'Therapeutic discourses', in *British Journal of Psychotherapy*, 12 (4), 447–460.

—— (1997) 'The unconscious state of social psychology', in Ibanez, T. and Iniguez, L. (eds), *Critical Social Psychology*, London: Sage.

Parker, I. and Shotter, J. (eds) (1990) *Deconstructing Social Psychology*, London: Routledge.

Parker, I. and Spears, R. (eds) (1996) *Psychology and Society*, London: Pluto Press.

Parker, I., Georgaca, E., Harper, D., McLaughlin, T. and Stowell-Smith, M. (1995) *Deconstructing Psychopathology*, London: Sage.

Piontelli, A. (1992) *From Fetus to Child*, London: Routledge.

Riley, D. (1983) *War in the Nursery*, London: Virago.

Rose, N. (1985) *The Psychological Complex*, London: Routledge and Kegan Paul.

—— (1989) *Governing the Soul*, London: Routledge.

Rose, N. and Miller, P. (1992) 'Political power beyond the State: problematics of government', in *British Journal of Sociology*, 43 (2), June.

Ryle, G. (1949) *The Concept of Mind*, London: Penguin.

Saussure, F. de (1974) *Course in General Linguistics*, London: Fontana.

Scott, W.R. (1937) *Adam Smith as Student and Professor*, Glasgow.

Segal, H. (1986) 'Notes on symbol formation', in *The Work of Hanna Segal: Delusion and Artistic Creativity and Other Psychoanalytic Essays*, London: Free Association.

Seve, L. (1978) *Man in Marxist Theory*, Sussex: The Harvester Press.

Sinason, V. (1988) 'Smiling, swallowing, sickening and stupefying: the effect of sexual abuse on the child', in *Psychoanalytic Psychotherapy*, 3 (2), 97–111.

—— (1992) *Mental Handicap and the Human Condition*, London: Free Association.

Smith, A. [1776] (1970) *The Wealth of Nations*, Skinner, A. (ed.), London: Penguin.

—— [1759] (1982) *The Theory of Moral Sentiments*, Raphael, D.D. and MacFie, A.L. (eds), Indianapolis: Liberty Classics.

126

Smith, D. (1988) 'Femininity as discourse', in Roman, L.G., Christian-Smith, L.K. with Ellsworth, E., *Becoming Feminine: The Politics of Popular Culture*, Sussex: Falmer Press.

Spinoza (1989) *Ethics*, London: J.M. Dent and Sons.

Tolman, C.W. (1994) *Psychology, Society, and Subjectivity*, London: Routledge.

Tolman, C.W. and Maiers, W.M. (eds) (1991) *Critical Psychology*, Cambridge: Cambridge University Press.

Tustin, F. (1994) 'Autistic children who are assessed as not brain-damaged', in *The Journal of Child Psychotherapy*, 20 (1), 105–131.

—— (1994a) 'The perpetuation of an error', in *The Journal of Child Psychotherapy*, 20 (1), 3–22.

Urwin, C. and Sharland, E. (1992) 'From bodies to minds in childcare literature', in Cooter, R. (ed.), *In the Name of the Child*, London: Routledge.

Varma, V.P. (ed.) (1992) *The Secret Life of Vulnerable Children*, London: Routledge.

Vygotsky, L.S. (1978) *Mind in Society*, Cambridge, Mass.: Harvard University Press.

—— (1986) *Thought and Language*, Cambridge, Mass.: MIT Press.

Walkerdine, V. (1988) *The Mastery of Reason*, London: Routledge.

—— (1990) *Schoolgirl Fictions*, London: Verso.

White, M. (1989) 'The externalizing of the problem and the re-authoring of lives and relationships', in Externalizing the Problem, *Dulwich Centre Newsletter*, summer 1988–1989, Adelaide.

White, M. and Epston, D. (1990) *Narrative Means to Therapeutic Ends*, New York: W.W. Norton.

Williams, D. (1992) *Nobody Nowhere*, London: Doubleday.

Williams, R. (1976) *Keywords*, London: Fontana.

—— (1987) *Culture and Society 1780–1950*, London: Hogarth Press.

Young, R. (1989) 'Transitional phenomena: production and consumption', in Richards, B. (ed.), *Crises of the Self: Further Essays – Psychoanalysis and Politics*, London: Free Association.

Index

The E-Business C
Coombs Wood R
Halesowen
West Midlands, B